Good Girl's Guide

to

Life after High School

By Lenore Craven

The names of the girls mentioned in this book have been changed to protect their privacy.

Book design by Lenore Craven

Cover design by Robb Hanks

Printed in the United States of America

For information regarding special discounts for bulk purchases, please contact our Sales department via fax at 1-866-585-0295 or via www.lenorecraven.com.

For Camille, who needs this now.

For Miranda, who will need this later.

For Dax, without whom this would never have been.

Preface

The Young Women's Program is a divinely inspired institution geared to help girls lay the foundations for adult life. Young Women's provides an opportunity for much spiritual, social, educational and emotional growth, ideally preparing women for the next step in their eternal progression: temple marriage. By the time you graduate from Young Women's, you are well-equipped with the tools needed to work towards a temple marriage. When you get your hard-earned medallion, you know your next major life goal: kneeling at the altar of the temple. But do you know how to get there and what to do along the way?

After Young Women's and high school, the gospel has taught you that the next step in eternal progression is eternal marriage. Anyone who has ever seen that three white dresses painting by Bernie Tanner understands the expectations. The first dress is the blessing gown; the second is the baptismal dress. That's eight years between white dresses, minimum. What about that last dress? Who knows how long it'll be before you get to zip up your bridal gown? This manual is to help you figure out what to do during those years between Young Women's and marriage – to assist you in making your life fulfilling and happy by setting goals for the pre-marriage years.

Getting married and having a family are top priorities, but developing your own life is part of realizing your full potential. And to think these potentially fabulous years are glossed right over in the three white dresses picture! While I don't discount the poignancy of Tanner's painting, there are plenty of other fantastic dresses you can wear in between these three white dresses. Between age 18 and marriage will be some of the most fun years of your life! The sassy, strappy party heels you get to wear between baptism and marriage are probably stuffed under the bed out of sight!

Latter-day Saint Women are groomed to be married. We are taught every skill imaginable to make us into lovely wives and mothers. Lessons from Primary through Young Women's and Relief Society include guidance on the perfecting of womanhood – an immensely worthy endeavor. We modern women hardly stop at the self-improvement courses designed for women by the Church; we are also encouraged to pursue formal higher education and careers. We have a thousand talents, a myriad of skills, and heaps of knowledge. We even have the desire and drive to be excellent Saints. Making ourselves the best women we can be is part of God's plan, and it's a wonderful one. The Father also invites us to be married in his temple and to eventually have children. There is a catch, however. We have to take a man along with us.

From the time we are divided into boys' and girls' classes at the ripe young age of 12 we were secretly being taught how to be wives and mothers. If I sound a little suspicious, it's because I am. The classes were never blatantly called "Wife Classes" – they were social activities where we could make friends. And cookies. And quilts. It's the quilts that really put me over the edge, even then. My brothers never had to make quilts. My grandmother twists in her grave when she hears them called quilts, as they are in fact ramshackle tied numbers that don't technically involve quilting at all. Furthermore, I can buy quilts for less than it costs to make them. But I digress.

We are trained to know how to cope when we get stuck with a man. We can make beds, paint Easter decorations, give CPR, and feed our families. I could probably manage to sew a man's mouth shut after having crammed it with homemade cookies, but no one ever taught me how to support myself and get married.

Where Laurel's leaves off and Institute hardly fills in, there will you find use for the *Good Girl Goals*. We're going to look at how one develops into adulthood personally, religiously, educationally, financially, and just generally. Our objective here is to make women the complete package – all the brains, beauty, and spirituality a woman needs to become an excellent marital prospect.

Take shoes, for example.

I love shoes. Shoes are the one factor that can make or break an outfit. Shoes instantly dress up a pair of jeans or dress down a skirt. Whatever else you're wearing, shoes tie everything together. They balance an outfit and communicate effort, all the while being functional and necessary. Cheap or expensive, heels or sneakers, shoes are great. I apologize ahead of time for my preoccupation with footwear, and I continue to repent for my wicked shoe-coveting ways, but shoes are important.

Shoe selection can be a metaphor for life. Ever seen a business woman on lunch wearing sneakers? She's dressed for her job, but leaves the office in tennis shoes to run some errands? That is an example of shoes ruining an outfit. When comfort and ease become the priority, your outfit ends up a disaster. And so it is with life and the living the gospel – neither is easy. If you're a well-dressed genius but you've neglected your spirituality, you're in no place to find a husband. If you're self-sufficient and spiritual but haven't bothered with education, your outfit could use improvement. Finding your correct balance of education, occupation, beautification, socialization and spirituality makes you ready for marriage. If you leave your house looking for a husband and have neglected one of these vital areas that complete a woman, you've made a life *faux pas*. My aim is to make this outfit we call life the best it can be for you during your early twenties.

That's where this manual comes in. It's a guide to being happy before you're married, and it worked for me. Some of the ideas are a bit radical, but as modern LDS women we need to take life by the reins and make it work for us. Getting married is an important goal of your twenties, so are getting educated, having a job, and being a contributing member of society. Sheri Dew has paved the way for unmarried sisters – being single is not a doomed fate. It's an opportunity for a life of your own. You never know what Heavenly Father has in store for you, maybe you'll get married next week or next half a century, or even in the next lifetime, but if you put all your ducks in a row you can be happy and single for as long as Heavenly Father wills. Learning how to be a

happy adult requires filling your reservoir full of life experience.

The Well of Life

Remember the OT story of Rachel at the well? Rachel was in the right place at the right time, she was "beautiful and well favored,"[i] and she had a job caring for her dad's sheep. Rachel was doing what she was supposed to do: drawing water at the well to feed her sheep. When Jacob rolled into town and saw Rachel, it was love at first sight: "And Jacob kissed Rachel, and lifted up his voice, and wept."[ii] I still can't believe that Rachel let him kiss her five minutes after they'd met, but that's how the story goes (and you can recite it to anyone who thinks kissing on the first date is a no-no). Jacob decides that Rachel is going to be his wife. Very little deliberation, no wasted time – Jacob just knew she was the right one, and apparently Rachel agreed. Jacob waltzed on over to her dad, Laban, and asked for Rachel's hand in marriage. Laban told Jacob that he could marry Rachel after Jacob worked for him for seven years. Jacob signed right up.

After seven years of slaving away for Laban, Jacob requested that Laban honor their agreement. That night, while Jacob waited for Rachel to come to him, Laban sent Rachel's big sister, Leah, instead. Now it's hard to imagine that Jacob would be fooled but they didn't have streetlights at the time. You can bet Jacob didn't see that one coming. The following day, Jacob was understandably mad and asked Laban again for Rachel. Laban told Jacob that marrying Rachel was going to take another seven years of work.

Amazingly, Jacob agreed again! You'd think the guy was nuts, but Jacob is the same guy whose name changed to Israel and became the father of the twelve tribes of himself. Sure, the man has peoples and a country eventually named after him, but marrying Rachel was obviously very important. Fourteen years after they first met at the well, Jacob finally got to marry Rachel.

Now, I ask you, what kind of girl was Rachel that Jacob would be willing to wait fourteen years to marry her? Even if Rachel was just sixteen when they met (people marry young in the Bible) she would have been thirty when they were finally married. What on earth was Rachel doing during those fourteen years? What did she have that made her "well-favored" and caused Jacob to fall for her hard enough that he would put up with such a sneaky father-in-law?

Rachel must have been something special; Heavenly Father needed her to be worth Jacob's labors so that they could go on to have children of infinite importance to the world. Do you know who one of Rachel's sons turned out to be? Donny Osmond. Okay, well actually Joseph, but Donny played him in the musical. That's right, Dreamcoat Joseph, sold into Egypt.

Whatever Rachel had, she was worth working for. But even if she was great enough to make Jacob kiss her and weep the first time they met, she still had fourteen years to kill before she got hitched. What do you think Rachel did with that time? My guess is she drew from the well of life!

You have no idea when Heavenly Father will send you someone to marry. In the time that you have before HF gives you a husband, you need to make yourself the best candidate for the best man out there.

Rachel was a supreme *Good Girl* – she was patient and worth waiting for. This text is structured as a list of goals that should be tackled before you tie the knot with some lucky guy. It takes a really *Good Girl* to go to the temple and get married. Being a *Good Girl* is hard! It's easy to be bad and break the rules, but being a *Good Girl* will ultimately get you what you want in life. The *Good Girl Goals* will guide you toward being ready for a temple marriage. Not everything in life can be achieved sequentially; you may be working on a number of goals at the same time and the man of your dreams might stroll by at any time.

The chapters are arranged according to how I experienced my post-YW years and follow the sequence in which I got my life in order as I worked toward making myself marriage material. The first thing I decided was that I was not ready to get married right after Young Women's. You have a lot of work ahead of you: you need to plan your education and your career. You need to live in the right place and find hobbies. You need to solidify your testimony, figure out if you should go on a mission, learn to control your hormones and be as beautiful physically and spiritually as you can be. Once you've laid some good foundations for adulthood, you need to have a strategy for finding a man and a checklist of what you expect from in a potential husband. It sounds like a lot of work, but it's also a whole lot of fun. Welcome, ladies, to the glory years!

In each chapter you'll read true stories of my Sisters in the gospel, including my biological sisters' experiences and those of the women I have known and observed, as well as several of my own personal experiences. All of the stories contained are based on real people, but their names and specific details have been changed. Many stories are warnings used as examples of how to avoid pitfalls during the rollercoaster that is Young Single Adulthood; many are inspiring illustrations of how women overcame obstacles in their path toward temple marriage. The stories are assembled in order to create a working guide of accumulated knowledge intended to help you figure out how to enjoy your twenties and achieve the goal of temple marriage. The theories conveyed are developed through my own interpretation of counsel from LDS Authorities, backed up with references from conference talks, Ensign articles, and other highly regarded sources. What with the people I've known and the guidance I've read from the Prophet and his counselors, I found there to be a deep well of experience from which a gal can draw.

If you follow the goals outlined in this guide, your twenties can be years of self-fulfillment, beauty and societal contribution. The goals provide training and experience from which you will be able to draw when you're a wife and mother. You can be college educated and career oriented as preparation for being an excellent mother[iii]; being accomplished is compatible with the tenants of the gospel. Your Heavenly Father wants you to maximize your potential on earth, married or not. Stick with me, honey, and you'll be well on your way being attractive and successful on a variety of levels. Yes, these things can be taught. Let's learn from the successes of other women who have chosen to reap the great opportunities available to a single woman. While you're drawing at the well of life experience, maybe your own Mr. Righteous will show up. Meantime, though, let's go make you into a *Good Girl*.

Good Girl Goal #1: Be the New LDS Bride

Lucy went to college at BYU Idaho and met her future husband (Joey) within six months. Like her mother Candace, Lucy got married at eighteen rather than finishing school. For a wedding present, the in-laws bought Lucy and Joey a new home in Idaho Falls. Lucy sits in her big house, bored and alone. Sometimes Lucy e-mails her high school friends, but most of them have moved on with their lives and have new friends they met in college. Lucy's daily life consists of waking up around ten, watching some daytime television, going to the mall and waiting to get pregnant. When her husband gets home from work, all Lucy has to tell him is that Macy's is having a sale on pie plates.

So, did Lucy win the jackpot? For some women this might sound like a dream come true: Lucy is married, she can go shopping any time she wants, and doesn't have to work. I would like to suggest an alternative approach to life. To begin, we're going to discuss the social expectation that LDS women should marry early. We will then look at statistics regarding young marriages and attempt to relieve some of the pressure to marry as soon as possible after high school. Finally, we'll talk about some reasons to wait a little while before tying the knot. Everybody knows a young bride like Lucy. Conceivably, Lucy's set up for a rather painless existence. She has it all figured out, right?

Think again, ladies! The world has more for you! The New LDS Bride is educated, employed, and self-sufficient with a solid testimony and magnificent shoes. The New LDS Bride lives where she wants, has friends of all colors and creeds, and is constantly busy with a myriad of hobbies and interests. The New LDS Bride has been places and done things, and she will marry on her terms!

Gone are the days when marriage is the only form of success for women. Write a thank you note to Mary Wollstonecraft, Virginia Woolf, Susan B. Anthony, the Suffragettes, and even good ol' Jane Fonda. These women have paved the way for you to get out of the kitchen and into a university where you can choose any career you wish (including right back into the kitchen, if we so please!) Women have grand opportunities available right now. Take advantage of them and distract yourself from the pressure to get married. Get an education! Travel! Pay your own bills! Have a job, have ten jobs! Make friends! Move! You're only young and single for a limited amount of years, but you have an eternity to be married. Make the best of your post-Young Women's years and marriage will fall into your lap when the Lord wills it.

Marriage is a fine institution, but I'm not ready for an institution![iv]

The four years between 18 and 22 are the foundation of your adulthood. They are some of the most interesting years of life and some of the most formative. During this time, the world is open to you – it's the time when you pick a college, choose a degree, figure out what you're passionate about, and pursue a career that will define your future participation in society. These are things that are best done alone. Not entirely alone, have as many friends and paramours as your heart desires. But c'mon, don't get married when you've just freed yourself from your parents' confines.

It's a common LDS view that girls should get married young, but why should we feel like old maids at age 22? The median age of marriage for a female in this country between the years 2000-2003 was 25.1 years. In the Appendix you will find a table showing the median (which means middle, for those of us who failed math) age of people first married in the United States. Here, we see that the population of the greater United States gets married in their mid- twenties. Find your state and feel the pressure to marry young fade away.

The state with the lowest median marriage age is also the state wherein most LDS Single Women live. Why are so many LDS women getting married young? The apparent reason is so that they can have sex, but can we pause to question that for a moment? If a young woman is chaste and intends to remain so until marriage, don't you think she would have a reasonably good handle on her hormones by the time she's even 18? Why all of the sudden at around 20 do these women just wed 'em and bed 'em? Have their hormones welled up to overflow? I don't think so. It is not a biological necessity to have sex before your 25th birthday; rather, LDS women are culturally encouraged to marry young. The expectation that we will be married before the national median needs to be chucked out like last season's Ugg Boots.

Don't fret, ladies who aren't married by 22. You are doing just fine! We are the New LDS Bridal Movement and we will marry whenever we're good and ready!

Here's what you say to your mother when she starts asking about your marriage prospects: "The national median for women to get married is 25. You are permitted to ask me about my marriage prospects one month after my 25th birthday and not sooner." Or better yet, threaten to move to Washington D.C. where the median age is 29.

Culturally, Mormon girls think that if they're not married by the time they're 22, they may have already blown their chance. Admit it. It's all right. You think about that one boyfriend that maybe would have fit the bill and probably you could have been happy.

Here's some information: everybody has an ex-boyfriend like that. You would have married him if you had wanted to get married, but you sabotaged the relationship somehow or another because it just wasn't right. So get over it.

When Naomi was eighteen, she had a boyfriend, Jonas, whom she absolutely loved. They dated, Jonas went on a mission, and Naomi wrote. Naomi was there waiting with open arms for him when he came home. Jonas and Naomi dated for awhile and then Naomi found herself talking to (alright, dating) other guys in her pottery class (see the "Make Yourself Interesting" Chapter). Jonas found out and dumped her. Naomi was heartbroken but eventually got married in the temple to Abel, a guy from her pottery class. Naomi still laments "losing Jonas" and frequently Googles him (see the "Showing Up on the Radar" Chapter) to see what happened in his life. She found out that Jonas got married to another woman, has a swarm of kids, and has an average job. He's perfectly happy. So is Naomi. Naomi has forgotten that she sabotaged the relationship in the first place and ended up with Abel who is a wonderful man who shares her interests and makes her perfectly happy.

Naomi and Jonas weren't right for each other, or maybe it wasn't the right time. We all have boyfriends like that and life goes on. We are free agents; we choose who we want to be with and when we want to get married. Until we get married, every dating relationship we have must end some time or another. Before you're married, *you have a 100% failure rate at dating.* However, we gain something from every relationship we experience. Even with the worst break-ups and heartaches, we are filling up our learning reservoirs. Everyone goes through painful break-ups. It's difficult to keep perspective, but being patient with HF and waiting for him to drop your husband in your lap is part of enduring to the end.

Moving on.

You don't have to get married right away. There are other goals to be accomplished before you get tied down. When you look back on your adolescence, I'm sure you can remember some really awkward years you've had. Unfortunately, the embarrassing years don't stop until you're about 21. After 21 (give or take late bloomers) you've established your adult personality. The four years between 18 and 21 are the adolescence of real adulthood. Those years are like adult puberty. You're on your own in college (yay!), you actually have to do your own laundry (boo!), and the bills come in your name (bigger boo!). Minus the acne and hormones (although, for me, they were still settling down, boo hiss!!) 18-21 are some rough years. It's going to take a few years to figure things out and you will make some mistakes. After 21, you don't think you're lame anymore. I don't know why, that's just how it is. So go ahead and get married AFTER 21.

Or you'll be sorry.

This is not speaking from personal experience; I waited well past 21 to get married, thank you very much. But Hannah faced the young marriage dilemma.

Hannah had this one boyfriend when she was 17-21. Oh, Sam was a cutie. T.D.H. (tall, dark, handsome), sincere, and would have made a great father. Sam was a few years older than Hannah. Hannah told me about going to the Bishop with Sam and that her Bishop said she and Sam should get married in 6 months. Hannah was only 19 and here she was with this huge choice to make. She'd never lived outside of the general area where she grew up and she had this boyfriend who seemed like a perfectly good marriage candidate whom she loved. They even bought a diamond ring together.

Later that week, Hannah skipped town. To this day, Hannah has no idea why she packed up all of her things and moved away to a college 300 miles away. Sam never forgave Hannah, but she told him that if they were going to get married, they could do it when she had her college degree.

Hannah had set that goal before she met Sam. She probably could have been perfectly happy with Sam, but she decided that she had a few more years to live single and to figure herself out. Hannah fully intended to marry Sam in a couple of years, but Sam was so angry with Hannah that he got mixed up with another girl and lost his temple recommend. Apparently, Sam's testimony was less sturdy than Hannah knew; it's even possible that Sam's behavior could have affected their marriage. The old maxim is: "If you love something, set it free. If it doesn't come back it was never meant to be." Hannah thinks she was guided away from Sam and she's never regretted her choices.

Hannah's life could have been very different with Sam as her husband. We should be thankful for all the near misses that help us juxtapose how our lives are and how they could have been.

Taking the Slow Lane to the Altar

I surveyed women who were married when they were 21 or younger, and all of them say variations of the same thing: "I wish I had a little more time as a single before getting married".

Ariel got married when she was nineteen. She never finished her college degree because she got pregnant. Though Ariel has a perfectly happy family life, she feels that she missed out on a complete college experience at that time in her life. Another lady, Candace, had a similar experience. She

decided to go back to school when she was forty-five. Good job, Candace.
However, Candace felt strange among all the young students and often did
not want to contribute in class because she thought she was too much of a
fish out of water.

Being married is not a bad thing (It's a great thing!!!), but life changes
when you get married. You're no longer a free individual; you're part of a pair.
You see, when you get married, you usually get pregnant shortly thereafter. My
mother used to threaten me with this saying, "Don't get married when you're in
school! You'll get pregnant! Your whole life will be devoted to your children!"
This is obviously not completely negative; having children is going to be
wonderful. But imagine all the things you can't do with children. You have to
travel with tons of luggage and cribs. You can't just bail on work and take the
kids out of school. You have to live in one place for a length of time to give the
kids an established home. Your husband will probably have to work harder to
support the family, especially if you're going to stop working. You might have
to pay for daycare. When you get married you usually have children within a
year or two and then your time is no longer your own. Women who marry
young must devote their lives to their husband and eventually their children. If
you ask the married women you know how long it was between their marriage
and their first kid, they will all tell you they wish they had had more time to
themselves.

More time to do what? Live their lives, I guess. How can they possibly reminisce about how great they were before they were married if they only had a year or so to themselves? Here's a challenge. Go find out how old five different women were when they were married. Ask them what they think about it in retrospect. Ask them when they had their first kid. Judge them accordingly, and then repent for judging them. Or skip the judgment and read some statistics I dug up. The Center of Disease Control did a study about divorce and its effects on health. The part about how divorce affects health was boring, but its conclusion regarding marriage age and divorce rate was interesting. According to a 2001 CDC study of 11,000 American women, "…younger age at marriage was associated with a higher probability of disruption. Of women who got married when they were younger than 18, almost two-thirds got divorced, compared with about a third of those married at age 20 or older".[v]

To sum up: married later, married longer. Better health. Everybody plays, everybody wins.

Good Girl Goal #2: Getting a Degree

What are you supposed to be doing with those four years between 18 and 21? Start with getting a degree. In this chapter, we're going to cover how education is part of the gospel, steps toward getting a college degree, choosing a school, figuring out how to pay for college, and considering options other than church schools. However you decide to go about getting an education, know that you have Gordon B. Hinckley's support: "Your first objective should be a happy marriage, sealed in the temple of the Lord, and followed by the rearing of a good family. Education can better equip you for the realization of those ideals."[vi]

I don't care how you do it or how long it takes you; you're going to need a bachelor's degree. Do it fast on loans or do it slow while working, but get your diploma. Here's why:

1. **It will make you better equipped to realize gospel goals.**

2. **You will never, ever feel comparatively intelligent without a college degree.**

It doesn't matter if you majored in gardening or jewelry making, if you have a college degree you feel smart. And you should! College infuses its graduates with a sense of accomplishment and equality. From personal experience, I can think of at least 3 women off the top of my head who have gone back to college after having dropped out when they were married (at BYU, no less). Why? Because they felt inadequate. They are great mothers and wives, and yet they felt this sense of inadequacy because they didn't have a degree. Everything your college counselor said to you while you were in high school to encourage you to get a college degree is important and true, but when all else fails, complete your schooling so that you can be a contributing educated member of society. Also, men think it's hot.

More on that: Everybody wants to marry someone smart so that they will have smart kids and also have someone more intelligent than a monkey hanging around their house. Why would a man want to marry someone with no education? Would you want someone buying shoes on your credit card who doesn't know how to balance a checkbook? (All right, I have no idea how to balance a checkbook). More applicable: Would you want someone buying a house on your credit that doesn't have a college degree? Sociologist Robert M. McIver said, "When you educate a woman, you educate a whole family." No man wants an uneducated woman raising his kids. Men want women who have self-worth and intelligence. Remember those Young Women Values? Self-worth was blue and knowledge was purple—both are delivered when that diploma is forked over.

Want to get married? Go get yourself a serving of self-worth. First thing you do? Get some schooling' and plan on getting a job.

Oh, here is what the prophet has said about it. GBH (that's shorthand for President Gordon B. Hinckley. My grandma grew up with him, so I entitle myself to use affectionate shorthand) addressed college-age students regarding the order of their priorities at that time in their life. His words are recorded in the May 1999 issue of the Liahona, in an article called "Life's Obligations." In this discussion he lists what he (the prophet, folks) recommends college student's priorities ought to be:

1. *To one's vocation.*
2. To one's family.
3. To the Church.
3. To one's self.

He even put the italics in there, helping to prove my first point. Rather than worrying about getting married, people who are of college age should worry about their vocation. **Vocation**, not to be confused with **vacation**, includes education with the intent to pursue a career. The second priority is family, and that includes your future family, next comes your Church involvement, and, finally, yourself. Your early twenties should be spent "cramming your heads with knowledge" to quote the Prophet. Here's what he says about a college education and career:

> **Choose a vocation where you will be happy. You will spend eight and more hours a day at it through all the foreseeable future. Choose something that you enjoy doing. Income is**

important, but you do not need to be a multimillionaire to be happy. In fact, you are more likely to be unhappy if wealth becomes your only objective. You will become a slave to it. It will color all your decisions. You need enough to get along on. You need enough to provide well for your family. It will be better if the husband becomes the provider and the wife does not work when children come. That situation may be necessary in some cases, but if you choose wisely now, it is not likely to become a requirement.

Choose a field in which you can grow. You need the stimulation of new effort and new ambitions, of new discoveries and new challenges.

Get all the schooling you can to qualify yourselves in your chosen vocations. In this world, competition is terrible. It eats up people. It destroys many. But it must be faced; it is something with which we have to deal.

Choose something that will be stimulating and thought-provoking and that will carry with it the day-to-day opportunity to do something to improve the society of which you will become a part.

These are the great days of your preparation for your future work. Do not waste them. Take advantage of them. Cram

your heads full of knowledge. Assimilate it. Think about it. Let it become a part of you.

I have something to add to the part about the man being the main provider. As a modern woman, I am required to balk at this antiquated perception of a working family; however, I believe the prophet's words that men should be the primary source of income, if possible. It is an old-fashioned way of thinking, but I buy it because the nurturer/provider paradigm has resulted in many a successful family. One of the best articles discussing the woman staying at home issue is "Wife and Mother: A Valid Career Option for the College-Educated Woman," which is a Brigham Young University Forum Address delivered April 3, 1979 by Sydney Smith Reynolds. I beg you to read the article because Sister Reynolds is brilliant. All the way back in 1979 (before I was even born, thank you very much) Sister Reynolds paved the way for highly educated and qualified women to feel confident in pursuing their education and a career outside of the home before they have children.

As it turns out, being a stay-at-home mother is the new feminist movement. After the sixties you were considered a feminist if you left home and got a job. Now, feminists and all sorts of professional woman are choosing to be stay-at-home moms and relishing every minute. Controversial findings in a recent study by W. Bradford Wilcox, sociologist at the University of Virginia, show that women "were happiest when their husbands were the main breadwinners for the family and when they did not work outside the home."[vii] More specifically, women found juggling children of school age and bringing home the bacon to be a miserable life. The prophets have championed that line of thinking for years. Raising children works best when women change careers from employee to CEO of the home, but that's not for a while off. This doesn't mean that you MUST leave your career when you become a mother; it just means that you have options and you can choose with impunity. We're celebrating choice and opportunity, not condemning working mothers. Meantime, developing your own foundation of education and career is both a resource and a fallback plan.

What this means to us is that we are no longer required to be barefoot in the kitchen cooking chicken pot pie, but we can choose that path if we want to! We can assign men to do the cooking and cleaning while we are teaching advanced chemistry at the local university. We have so many more choices than men; we get to raise our children if we want to. And you better believe I'll be pushing that stroller in fantastic high heels.

Smart Girls Go To College

When I say get an education, I mean formal education. I mean a professional or Bachelors degree, maybe even an MA, LLM., MBA, or a PhD. There are many pathways to becoming and educated person. Moreover, you can start your education at any time: people who live the gospel are already adept at being lifelong learners and formal education may be approached the same way. Two helpful ways to choose your educational path are to either decide to study whatever your favorite subject was in high school, or pick a job and figure out a path to getting that job.

For the job path, the best way to figure out how to get into a specific profession is to ask someone in that field what sort of education is required. Ask them what they studied and where. This is generally flattering and you shouldn't have too much trouble figuring out how to become whatever it is you want to be. Research the job online as well. Picking your favorite subject in high school and running with that can be just as rewarding. If you liked learning French, learn some more and work towards a career in translation. If you only liked P.E., go study Kinesthetics because it's just a fancy name for Physical Education. High school was designed to be foundational and to expose you to a lot of fields of learning, when you get to college, the areas simply become more specific. Some schools offer courses in everything from crime scene investigation to floral arrangement. Whatever you dig, there's a class out there for you.

There is a college experience for every personality. Most college search websites provide a custom option through which you can outline what you want in a college, such as size, tuition amount, location, type of school, and majors offered. You can even see if the school offers night or online courses and degrees. These sites will help narrow down your college search. I recommend www.collegenet.com and www.collegeboard.com for four year schools. However, doing all four years at a University is not always the best option. That's why the government invented community colleges.

The Community College Option

Getting a bachelor's degree can be a two-step process and if you've neglected to apply for college when most people do during their junior year of high school, that's perfectly alright. Going to a local community college is an inexpensive way to pursue an education, whether you're working full-time or going to class full-time. The two-year unfairly named "Junior College" is a perfectly viable and affordable option for beginning, returning to, or adding on to your education. Anyone can go to community college; these colleges promote ongoing education and lifetime learning. Here's some history about community colleges (I chose California's because it was one of the first, but nearly every state has a Community College system):

> In 1907 the California Legislature, seeing a benefit to society in education beyond high school but realizing the load could not be carried by existing colleges, authorized the state's high schools to offer what were termed "postgraduate courses of study" similar to the courses offered in just the first two years of university studies. In 1917 the Junior College Act was passed, expanding the mission by adding

trade studies such as mechanical and industrial arts, household economy, agriculture, and commerce.[viii]

Community colleges around the United States have similar histories and intentions. Community colleges have an open enrollment policy, which means anyone can go. The highest degree awarded to students at a community college is the Associate's Degree. All two-year "postgraduate" (as in, from High School) programs have an Associates as the highest degree, this includes art schools and technical schools for computers and the like.

Why Community Colleges are a Good Choice

1. Same education as the first two years at a four year school.

2. Fraction of the cost.

4. Many, many people attend them.

5. Easy to transfer as a junior to a four year school.

6. More flexible for examining possible majors.

7. You can start whenever you want and go to community college indefinitely.

8. You can switch schools when you move with little or no penalty.

9. Classes are often fairly easy.

10. Many courses are offered at night.

11. Smaller class size.

There! Ten good reasons to go to a community college for the first two years of higher education.

This Girl's Life:

When I graduated from High School, I went straight to one of the University of California campuses. After one term there, I realized I could get the same education in smaller classes for less money at a Community College (CC). I left my four year college and enrolled the next semester at a CC. When I felt like moving, I moved and went to a new CC. Eventually, I transferred to another UC that I liked a lot better than the first. I still graduated in the traditional four years and have never been asked if I went to a CC because I have a four year degree from a University of California. I turned out fine.

The application process for a CC and four year schools are fairly straightforward and the college websites have plenty of information. Applications always cost a completely disproportionate amount of money but *c'est la vie.* (Harvard collects an estimated $1 million dollars just off application fees. Evil!) Use the college search websites to choose a school and then make a plan of getting there, whether you are applying directly or going first through a CC.

If you choose to do the CC route, the first thing you should do is meet with a college counselor. Tell the college counselor where you eventually want to go or be and ask them how to get there. Usually the CC will have a pathway for every major and the courses needed as a foundation for a Bachelor's or technical degree. The pathways are educational plans called something like a transfer agreement. The one I encountered most frequently was the Intersegmental General Education Transfer Curriculum, or IGETC. These, plus a few classes directly relating to your field of choice will provide the foundation for getting you into a four-year college. Most transfer requirements should be able to be completed in two years.

When you get accepted to any school, the first thing you do is officially enroll, which is a process not unlike immigration. You get a student number, ID, etc. They throw you a makeshift map and send you on your way. After you enroll, you register for classes. Ask anyone in the Admissions Office about enrollment. They will direct you. Rather than having your mother walk you through registration, take some initiative and speak with the Admissions Office because every school is different. Don't worry about looking lost or asking stupid questions because they've seen a million other students march through this rigmarole. Next, go to class, study hard, get good grades, and graduate. **There is no good reason for you to draw out your education unnecessarily.** You should be able to get through a typical Bachelor's program in four years. Notice the use of the word "get" in association with "an education." Getting an education is a proactive activity; it doesn't just fall into your lap. You have to ask questions, do your research, and work hard to get good grades. Make good use of your educational time. Soak it in. Yes, you're paying for it, but it's an excellent investment.

Good Girl School Choices

The first thing you need to do when you're choosing a college is decide what interests you. What do you actually enjoy doing? What type of shoes do you prefer to wear? What subjects did you enjoy in high school? What could you stand learning about for a minimum of two years? You might want to skip ahead to "Girl's Gotta Work" and see if something sticks out. Your major can be a foundation for a career or completely unrelated. You can do more than one major at a time, and you can add as many minors as you want. College is flexible like that.

School rankings in your particular area of study can help you choose a school. Other factors that you should consider are listed on any college search engine, for example, the College Board website. If you go to their "Find Colleges" page, you'll find a page that narrows your college search first by picking the Type of School, Location, Majors/Academics, Campus Life, Activities and Sports, Admissions, Financial Aid, and Deadlines. Imagine picking a school just because they have a great ice-hockey team. That's how specific these searches can get, and you can choose your college based on the factors most important to you. Sometimes it comes down to that sort of non-academic information – maybe both the schools you like have good Geology departments but only one of them has a good swim team. There are more than 3,600 schools to choose from.

Location is important. Where you chose to go will determine the type of footwear you will be required to wear and your college lifestyle. When I went to UC Santa Cruz, the footwear of choice was hiking boots because of the lack of paved paths and rain. In New York, you will have to walk a considerable amount but also wear fashionable shoes. Tennis shoes are all right for daytime in San Francisco and galoshes are best for Seattle. Provo may require snowshoes, as will Denver and Chicago. The college search sites will help match your preferred lifestyle (and shoe style) to the perfect location with questions like "rural, suburban, or urban?" These websites guide you through what type of school to consider and broaden your horizons from just the schools you've heard of or the ones your family prefers. The size of the school matters too, as does cost of tuition, and housing. All of these factors are important to making an informed college choice.

Choosing where to go to college is probably is arguably one of the most important decisions of your adult life. . Don't let anything stop you from going to the University of your dreams, whether or not it is a church school. The more information you have about your school before you start shelling out cash, the better your experience will be. Apply to as many as you want to. Apply to long shots. Try going somewhere new. This is the perfect time in your life to experience a new world, and college can be just that opportunity.

How Am I Gonna Pay For This?

Not all of us are lucky enough to have familial financial support through college. Some families do have the resources and still expect students to pay their own way, figuring that the education is more valuable if it is self-funded. Either way, the U.S. encourages citizens toward higher education by making money available through loans, grants, and work opportunities.

It is in the government's best interest to have well-educated citizens because well-educated citizens are more likely to earn large sums of money and improve the infrastructure of the general economy. The college-educated are usually productive members of society, are more likely to follow laws, and educated communities are generally safer. For these reasons, borrowing money for education is both respectable and encouraged. And don't worry; you won't have to pay all the money back the day you graduate. Perfectly sane people borrow money for school and pay it back gradually for ten to twenty years after they graduate. Educational debt is one kind of good debt, and it is understood that people must borrow a reasonable amount to cover education expenditures. The BYU Financial Aid website quotes the Prophet thus, "I urge you to be modest in your expenditures; discipline yourselves in your purchases to avoid debt to the extent possible. Pay off debt as quickly as you can, and free yourselves from bondage ... shrink expenditures to fit the income . . ."[ix]

Only borrow what you need to live, not what you need to buy this season's Guess boots and Christmas presents for everyone you know. All schools offer some sort of Financial Aid program, but the first thing you will be required to do is fill out a FAFSA form.

FAFSA is a less than clever acronym for Free Application for Federal Student Aid (it should be FAFFSA, but nobody listens to me). The website is listed below, but just type FAFSA into any search engine online and all the information is available in a step by step process. This application gets the ball rolling on Federal Stafford Loans, which function to cover the cost of tuition for you depending on your eligibility. If year's tuition, for example, costs $10,000, they might pay $6,000 and you would be responsible for the other $4,000. The rest of the money you can cover by private loans or grants. When filling out the FAFSA, the government will ask you all kinds of information about you and your family's financial history, including how much your parents make. This always bugged me because if you were legally claimed as a dependent on your parent's tax forms then you have to include a lot of their information which can decrease the amount you're given. I think the theory is that if your parents have money, they want to give priority to students who don't have potential external resources. Makes no sense to me, because even if your parents can pay for school, they may not and then you may not quality for financial aid based on their annual income. You can prepare for this potential problem by talking to your parents about not claiming you on their tax forms.

Filling out the FAFSA also gauges your financial need for Pell Grants. You are lucky if you get a Pell Grant because you never have to pay it back! It's free money for school! The applications for FAFSA are due every year around June and require a yearly update. After the FAFSA, private loans are also available as are grants. The best way to access money for education is to go to your University's Financial Aid department and they will walk even the most clueless person through borrowing money and/or applying for grants. Typically, the resources available will be Federal Stafford Loans (FAFSA), short term loans given by some colleges, and Pell Grants. Also available are private grants for just about everything; if you're 1/8th Mongolian and 3/16ths Nigerian, I'm sure there's a grant for that. There are clown school grants, smarty pants grants, and grants for whale watching. If you're wily, you can find a grant for just about anything by doing searches on the Internet or asking your university. Your university can also guide you through how to access private educational loans through your bank. The people at the university are getting paid to help you pay for college. They expect you to know nothing, so don't be afraid to make an appointment before you show up to start school.

Thinking Outside the Church School Box

The LDS church is so supportive of education that they even went so far as to establish and operate full-time universities. You may have heard of them. They're called BYU and its affiliates. Just so you know before you get there, BYU- Provo is ranked 71 on US News and World Report Best National University of 2006. If you're bright enough to get into BYU, it's not a sin to consider other Universities. The school from which you choose to graduate has great impact on the rest of your academic life as well as your career. Many employers don't much care where you graduate as long as it's a four year school. Most LDS students (and their pushy parents) want to go to BYU because it's cheap. Well, I guess you could say it's cheap, but you've been paying for it as long as you have been paying your tithing. Part of church tithing is paid to support church education, an obviously worthy endeavor. Tithing helps keep the cost of tuition at BYU low as 70% of the school's costs are funded by member's tithing whether your family goes there or not. Tuition is around $3,500, and room and board in lovely Provo is about $5,600 a year, thereby ranking BYU- Provo at 22 on the US News "Best Value" list.[x] Tuition is low, education is good, you're surrounded by LDS students, and can be sure that your roommate is not going to bring home drugged up vagabonds (unless they manage to escape from nearby Provo Canyon School, the local celebrity rehab joint.) These are the main reasons why LDS students are encouraged to go to BYU, Provo, Hawaii or Idaho.

Why, then, do out of state parents send their students who don't get into BYU to Utah Valley State College or the University of Utah? They're not church subsidized, the fees for UVSC out of state tuition are around $9,500, and the education is ranked in the lower third tier of colleges. University of Utah is ranked 120 on the Best National Schools list and costs a cool $13,000 out-of-state tuition. Why are these the back-ups if you don't get into BYU? If you're a resident of Utah, they are great options. However, if you live in just about any other state, I urge you to consider a state school. They'll be cheaper.

To be fair, Utah does offer some features that you just can't get anywhere else: specifically, mass majorities of Mormons. Going to an LDS school may put you in contact with the most concentrated supply of young single members you will ever experience. In August of 2005, 54.6% of the individuals in the graduating class at BYU were married.[xi] Since my parents met at BYU, I can't condemn choosing a school based on the probability that you will get married before you graduate. However, going to a church school does not mean that your husband is waiting for you there. Remember what GBH said? Education should come first at this time in your life. If you get into a highly-ranked school outside of Utah and choose to attend a less prestigious school in the Beehive State you may regret the decision. Very few people in the working world (other than LDS members) have heard of Utah schools other than BYU, so having a degree from those schools will not be as valuable when you're applying for jobs. Make sure to ask yourself how you feel about attending school where everyone has the same foundation of belief. It may seem like a promised land with fields of handsome temple recommend-holding men, but it also may cramp your style and make you feel like a face in the crowd of blushing Mormon girls. Utah means serious competition and men often get kinda spoiled by the bevy of beautiful women and have trouble committing to just one.

To Provo or Not To Provo?

There are many ways to experience a church school. Because you and I already know the reasons why someone would want to go to BYU, I've chosen instead to include a less traditional opinion from Daniel, a BYU graduate.

After my mission, I wanted to go to BYU to get married. I had attended Yale before my mission, but my Mission President said that I ought to get married as soon as possible. To heed this good advice, I thought BYU would be my best bet. I received an excellent education at BYU, but before you decide to go, you have to sit down and ask yourself some questions.

You're signing up for a university experience where General Authorities regularly come to hold devotionals. You say prayers in classes. It's a safe, regimented environment. Here's what you have to delineate: BYU is a place where your freedom of choice will be drastically limited if you want to remain a student there. Some people say that when you go there you lose the freedom to choose, which I think is untrue. You've made a choice by enrolling and signing the BYU Honor Code. When you choose to go there you have to abide by the Honor code, a code which is not synonymous to everyday Mormon life. You're held to a stricter standard of living at BYU. This can be hard to wrap your head around because you're used to a certain hands-off personal honor code that's between you and the Lord. When you're at BYU you're held to a certain set of rules that are unique to BYU, namely the length your hair can be, facial hair restrictions (hopefully not a problem for girls), white glove cleaning inspections, and no one of the opposite sex venturing beyond the kitchen or commons area in your apartment to the bedrooms beyond. What you're signing up for is an education that is intrinsically and intricately interlocked and connected with religion.

I think you need to carefully and prayerfully consider that. Yes, it's a target rich dating environment. Many of the most eligible LDS men are at BYU and if that's your priority, it's great. But with those opportunities comes a lifestyle that you might not be accustomed to leading, you might not agree with, and it might cause you to become more rebellious than you naturally are. You can get a quality education at BYU. I did. But I didn't

meet the girl I was to marry until after college.

For many LDS women, college and marriage go hand in hand. I think this philosophy has cheated untold amounts of women out of a rewarding successful career and personal development. Consider interpreting the counsel of President Hinckley in this way: college should be your well-researched foundation for a productive and fulfilling career, not just a big meat market to get you married off before you have to support yourself.

Don't get me wrong, my parents both went to LDS schools, as did my siblings and my husband. There are plenty of excellent reasons for choosing an LDS school, but don't feel limited and don't go planning to get married. Many church leaders, mission presidents and families worry that LDS students will not get married if they don't go to LDS schools. However, the Church has thought of that and installed Institutes of Religion near just about every school in urban America. There are members everywhere; you can still marry someone wonderful if you don't go to a church school. Education is designed to prepare you to financially support yourself and be an informed member of community. If you're well-educated and can provide for a family if necessary, it won't matter how many eligible men there are in your town. You'll only have to take one under your well-educated wing. Good people go to church schools, but don't let your parents talk you into feeling guilty for not going to the Promised Land for your schoolin'. Besides, if you make it through a non-affiliated college without any serious prospects, you can always move to Utah later on to live, work, marry, and be merry.

Hey, Smart Guy

Just for your amusement, I researched the schools attended by the current Presidency of the Church and the Twelve Apostles. Bear in mind, many of these men were raised in Utah, so that may have influenced their choice of schools. Also, when these guys were of college age, the U of U was ranked higher than BYU. Maybe you should write them each a letter and ask them why they chose these schools. I hear they like getting letters.

Where Did the Leaders Go to College?

Gordon B. Hinckley	University of Utah
Thomas S. Monson	University of Utah, BYU
James Faust	University of Utah
Boyd K. Packer	Weber State, Utah State, BYU
L. Tom Perry	Utah State University
Russell M. Nelson	University of Utah
Dallin H. Oaks	BYU, University of Chicago
M. Russell Ballard	University of Utah
Richard G. Scott	George Washington University
Richard D. Hales	University of Utah, Harvard
Jeffrey R. Holland	Dixie, BYU, Yale
Henry B. Eyring	University of Utah, Harvard

| Dieter Uchtdorf | German Air Force, Arizona Flight School |
| David A. Bednar | BYU, Purdue |

While I was researching the educational history of our leaders, I went ahead and looked at the area authorities and the women currently in leadership positions. The General Relief Society President Bonnie D. Parkin got her Bachelor's at Utah State University, her counselor Anne C. Pingree holds a Bachelor's from U of U, and her other counselor Kathleen Hughes went Weber University and earned a Master's Degree at Central Missouri State University. All the other leaders of the church were ever more varied in their educational background. As a side note, I am always impressed by the high level of education of our Church Authorities. It boosts my testimony to see well-educated Saints. I'm anxious to see the educational history of our Authorities in the future. Diversity helps my testimony.

Resources:

- USNews.com has great up-to-date rankings information about all the Colleges in the US. It's fairly non-bias and gains no obvious profit.

- www.collegeboard.com Tells all about preparation and has college features search engine to help you choose which school.

- www.collegedirt.com Information about a college by the students. Fun.

- Your college counselor from high School, a counselor at any junior college, an admissions director at any college (for that college).

- "God on the Quad" by Naomi Schaefer Riley. This book is reviewed as an "even-handed" look at twenty different religious universities, including BYU.

- "The Gatekeepers: Inside the Admissions Process of a Premier College" by Jacques Steinberg. At www.deseretbook.com

- Paying for College without Going Broke by Kalman A. Chaney also at deseretbook.com

- *The Only Mormon in the Dorm* by Elizabeth S. VanDenBerge. Ensign, June 1990.

- www.fafsa.ed.gov

- BYU's website has an excellent description of financial options for students.http://saas-dev.byu.edu/depts/finaid/

Good Girl Goal #3: Is this the place?

If you live in the same area where you grew up, pack your high heels and move. Everybody needs to jump out of the nest sometime. It's time for you to get out of town, maybe even out of the state or country. I highly recommend moving somewhere where you don't know anyone at all just because you'll get to make all new friends.

Moving provides an added degree of independence. It may sound hard and scary, but the benefits are great. You get new friends, a new job, a new place to live, and you get to be the new girl from a different place. Change is good, and it will help with your marriage goal.

You can reinvent yourself every time you move and there is little or no negative stigma attached to girls who move around a lot. It's best to stay in each place one or two years so that your resume doesn't look so piecemeal. When you move to a different place you face a new set of challenges that will keep you busy so you can quit obsessing over the fact you're single.

Where Should I Move?

My friend Claudia is brilliant. She has a bachelor's degree, holds a temple recommend, works with autistic children, and is completely independent. Claudia is 29 and is whip smart. She has her head square on her shoulders and is very down to earth. Claudia isn't a beauty queen. She doesn't keep up with the local trendy fashion and recently learned the difference between yellow and pink concealers. She moved to a new city to pursue more education and to expand her social life. Here's where she picked: Los Angeles. Bad move Claudia! Didn't consider the competition! The girls in Los Angeles are younger, thinner, and generally less educated. The men who live there are typically accustomed to Jessica Simpsons running around. Go to the Los Angeles First Ward and assess who is engaged and who is not. The young, stunning girls go first and the well-educated, seasoned women sit around wondering why. Claudia lived in Los Angeles for about one year and then moved to Colorado where she met and married her husband within three months of moving. Well done!

Choosing where you're going to move must be strategic.

Here's what Claudia did: she assessed her local competition and moved somewhere where her best features would be appreciated. She is a well-traveled and a city girl, and these two features that made her a standout in the small Colorado town. Your strategy is two-fold: You can either move somewhere where there are men who share a similar world view and tastes (see *Good Girl*

Goal # 14), or you can move somewhere where you are the only person like you around for miles.

The stereotypes about regions in America generally hold some truth: San Francisco appreciates artistic, granola people who drive Hybrids. Colorado is for outdoorsy types. Boston is great from intellectual liberals, Seattle is grassroots, vegetarians. Chicago is no nonsense business types who like the cold, New York likes tough people, and Washington D.C. is where valedictorians hang out. Los Angeles is where lots of the popular kids from high school end up, for better or worse. These are, of course, gross generalizations but they do provide an idea of what you can expect when you move to these areas. You see it in movies all the time. Remember *Legally Blonde?* Sorority queen gets into Harvard and finds out she doesn't fit in? In the movie, Elle focuses on the part of her personality that is valued in that area: academic accomplishments. She gets married to a hot intellectual type.

This Girl's Life:

One moving strategy that works is moving to an area where they've never seen the likes of you before. That's what my husband did. He was a typical Boston liberal-intellectual, but he picked up and moved to Los Angeles. I spotted him wearing a scholastic blazer on a sunny LA day. I knew he probably was the breath of fresh air I'd been waiting for after dating movie industry people for two years. He said he wanted to marry someone who wore high heels.

Same thing happened with my friend Hazel. She wanted to marry someone who had a real job, wore sensitive sweaters, and had an impressive Indie music collection. So she moved to San Francisco. She is now happily married.

You are not defined by where you live. However, where you live may define what types of people surround you. People tend to move to a place where there are other people with their same priorities; that's why so many Mormons live in Utah. Want to marry someone who considers politics a viable career option? Move to the D.C. area. Sick and tired of wimpy men without any back bone and no job? Move to New York. Want to link up with an actor? Move to Los Angeles. These are, of course, gross generalizations but they do provide an idea of what you can expect when you move to these areas. You see it in movies all the time. Remember Legally Blonde? Blonde sorority queen gets into Harvard and finds out she doesn't fit in? In the movie Elle focuses on the part of her personality that is valued in that area: academic accomplishments. She gets married to a hot intellectual type.

Regardless of where you decide to go, take comfort in knowing that there are normal people living in any metropolitan area. One of the greatest features of the gospel is that it's true, no matter where you go. That means there will be kind saints to help you get situated wherever you end up, and you'll have a community no matter where you go. My best advice is move somewhere you find pleasing and desirable and have faith that your future husband will do the same thing.

Get New Digs

When you're moving to a new town, the first resource you should tap is the local ward. Just find the phone number for the local ward online at www.lds.org by going to the Stake and Ward website pages and conducting a search for your new area. For example, I typed in New Orleans and three wards came up, one of which is the Young Single Adults ward. That's what you need. The phone number listed should be to the bishop's office. Leave a message saying that you're moving to the area and need to find a place to live. Hopefully, someone will call you back and put you in contact with the ward housing coordinator who is in charge of compiling up-to-date information about roommate and apartment vacancies within the ward. If no one gets back to you, the ward building is a great place to stop by as soon as you get into town. Usually there are posting boards of people looking for LDS roommates. Contact them and check out the apartment.

I highly recommend living with LDS roommates because you are more likely to share common standards. Most girls who live in LDS apartments will not bring home random men, drugs, or big burning crosses. Being Mormon does not mean that they're going to be perfect, but hopefully some common expectation of decorum will be followed. The best part of living with LDS girls is that you'll always have someone to sit next to at church. LDS girls will share your social circle, so you'll have that added encouragement for you to get along with each other. The only major drawback to having LDS roommates is that sometimes you might want to date the same guys. You'll need to communicate and constantly remind yourself that these are your Sisters in the gospel. Take care of each other.

Renting Info

When you've picked an apartment, expect to fill out an application, pay a deposit, and sign a contract for 6 months to a year. Do not be afraid to negotiate the rental price and terms of the contract. Most managers will run a credit check, or you can bring one along with you in a sealed envelope to make the process go a little faster. There are three credit bureaus: Experian, TransUnion, and Equifax. New regulation now entitles you to a free credit report every year, so go to www.annualcreditreport.com or you can also call them at (877) 322-8228 and request your free credit report. Even if you've never had a credit card or bought anything on credit, you still get a report showing no activity, which is just fine. Occasionally, some landlords require a co-signer for your first apartment, especially if you don't currently have a job. Your co-signer should be someone who trusts you to pay the rent or someone who will back you up if you're short.

This is the worst part about moving. It costs a lot. Security deposits are commonly equivalent to first month's rent and need to be paid in cashiers checks or bank drafts (make sure to get a receipt). You can save yourself a lot of hassle with moving if you move into an established apartment where other girls already live and you're just replacing one of them on the lease. Deposits are for the landlord's security if the apartment is vacated without proper notice from you or you don't pay your rent. The landlord cannot keep your deposit unless you neglect to pay rent, move out without proper notice or break your lease agreement in any other way. There will also probably be a cleaning fee of less than $250.[xii] The landlord will use the cleaning fee for repainting, carpeting and repairs after you move out. Some states (California, for example) require that the landlord provide an itemized bill for cleaning and repairs. Feel free to check out all the renting requirements at your state's real estate website under the section regarding tenant's rights and obligations. In this case, it's possible to just take over the moving girl's contract by paying her what she paid for the deposit, but make sure you get your name on the lease contract so that when you all move out you can get your refund check from the management company.

Other than that, you should remember to keep copies of everything you give to the landlord and everything you sign. Keep a copy of your lease agreement on hand. Renting is fairly safe, but the odd management company can be a frustrating hassle. You should know the landlord must always tell you in advance if someone is going to be entering your apartment for any reason, you will be charged a fee for late rent, and you are generally not allowed to have overnight visitors stay for more than a specified amount of time. The landlord can kick you out (this is called "Eviction") for breaking or violating your lease, such as having pets without permission. And as I learned the hard way, always consult your landlord before you paint the walls pink. If you have any questions or concerns, keep good records and remember that letters on law firm letterhead are always effective (another good reason to date a lawyer).

You Mean I Have to Live With HER?

Living with roommates can be a delight or a real challenge because some will inevitably steal your shoes. I have lived with more women than I can remember, and it is always a unique learning environment. No apartment situation has ever been perfect, but the best lesson I learned was that you can only control yourself. No matter how challenging the roommate situation, if you maintain a Christ-like attitude you can get by. Everyone has different home experiences that they bring to a roommate situation; each person has different standards of cleanliness and lifestyle within the home. When you first move in, you may want to consider discussion of home standards so that you know exactly what to expect. House rules can be simple but need to be expressed so that future conflict may be avoided.

Good House Rules

Make sure they wear a different shoe size from you.

Do your own dishes.

Keep the common areas clean.

Ask if you're having guests stay over.

Mutually agree on quiet hours.

Be forewarned: girls are messy. Surprising, isn't it? Well, maybe not messy, but most are definitely "cluttery". We have a lot of stuff. When women move out of their family home, they frequently are not used to taking care of their own messes and it takes some adjustments. You probably leave clutter yourself. Be honest, it's okay. When you're just about to throw a fit and leave all of the dirty dishes on your roommate's bed, (okay, I did this once. Sorry, Diana!) try, try, try to remember that we're all learning and most roommate problems are not intentional.

Of course, there may be problems. These people are not your family and you might get mad at them for doing things you think are inconsiderate. Remember that your definition of clean and considerate may be different from others. Try not to take roommate problems personally and establish a functioning home environment through neutral conversation. Never make home problems public by complaining to your bishop or ruining other girls' reputations around the ward. Communicate.

Resources:

- Lisa Ann Jackson, "In Good Company," Ensign, Oct. 2003. Clear discussion on roommates and relationships.

- Susan Fee, <u>My Roommate is Driving Me Crazy! A survival guide for the inevitable</u>.

- www.apartmenttherapy.com - Website devoted to those of us living in tiny apartments. There's an annual contest for best use of space

- www.doctorjob.com - Advice and community for graduates.

- http://www.lds.org/units is the LDS Stake and Ward Website link. Find your new Ward!

Good Girl Goal #4: Good Girls Don't Take Handouts

It embarrasses me to quote Destiny's Child, but "All the women who are independent, throw your hands up at me." If you want people to take you seriously, quit taking hand-outs. We need to confront the issue of female self reliance and independence – how it applies to the gospel, how it can effect dating, and how you can prevent getting financially in over your head.

The Plan of Happiness and Paying Your Own Bills

The best reason to get a job is so that you can be self-sufficient. We'll talk about which job in the following chapter. Once you have a job, you will feel like a real human being. A job is power. After a year of a steady paycheck, you will never look back. There is little more satisfying than your payday pair of shoes or facial (other than gospel blessings, of course). And money isn't the only benefit; working makes you feel useful and gives you purpose in life, even if the purpose is only a stepping stone in your eternal life. Prophet Howard W. Hunter has my back on this one, too. He writes: "There are several principles which reinforce the significance of work in the Lord's plan. First, as the covenant people we must be as self-sufficient as possible. We are to be free from dependence upon a dole or any program that might endanger our free agency."[xiii]

Being self-sufficient is an element of the plan of happiness. We are free, which means we are free to support ourselves in the best way we see fit. When you have a job, you are free to take care of your own finances and can make your own decisions about how to spend your money. You can decide where and how to live. You can spend all of your money constructing an Oreo cookie tower or excavating ancient baboon burial grounds and no one could stop you.

Unless, of course, you've made a colossal blunder: you're living off your parents after you've graduated from college.

You have an education. You can get a career. Get off the teat.

That's right, I said it. Quit taking money from your parents, you mooch. Presents are fine, the odd haircut or shopping excursion, but there is no reason why you can't pay your own bills.

The Independent Dater

Men do not dig girls who are still on their parents' payroll after college. If your parents are paying your bills, your hotness goes down 10 points for every bill. I'll tell you why. When a man finds out the woman he's interested in is not paying her bills, it's a huge red flag. It demonstrates **her lack of ambition to be self sufficient and that she has to depend on other people to meet her financial needs**. If she's willing to take regular handouts from the people she loves, how much is she going to require from her new man? Would marriage for her be simply a transferring of the teat? Such women are seen by men as a liability. If you can't take care of yourself, how can you contribute to a marriage?

Further, financial dependence rattles other huge male fears to the surface: Is she only interested in me for my money? What kind of leech am I dating? Even if you don't mean to, the man will now see you as a girl who can't take care of her own business and is used to people doing things for her.

Basically, a spoiled brat.

If you are taking money from your parents, you need to reexamine your finances. Quit buying shoes, paint your own nails, and sell everything you own on e-bay, move in with roommates, move to a cheaper city, but do NOT siphon money from the parental unit for any purpose other than for emergencies.

This also includes living with your parents. Would you marry a guy who lives with his parents? Enough said. I don't care how cheap it is to live there – you're sabotaging your chance to get married. So pay up and move out.

When it comes to dating, men and women have different expectations as far as money and who pays. This can be a real challenge. Women are often raised to expect men to pay for them; men often expect to foot the bill for dates. However, in this casual era, these social constructs are outdated and limiting. Don't assume that ANYONE is going to take care of you but you. That means, when going on dates plan to pay for your own way. That said, you should be careful of guys who do not offer to pay. Yes, they're conflicting, but I'll explain.

"Dutch-dating" means that the bill is split in some way. If you're doing dinner and a movie, you can let him pay for dinner and you pay for the movie or vice versa. If he plans something extravagant, you are not obliged to reciprocate, but let him know that you are more interested in his company than his money. There is nothing more unattractive than a woman who refuses to contribute. At the very least, pay the tip or the valet.

When I was dating, splitting the bill caused a lot of problems. When I suggested to the guy that I wanted to contribute it often caused that fragile male ego to flare up, but it was always worth it because at the end of the date I felt less committed to the whole experience. If we both paid, then I could pretend we were just friends hanging out casually. As soon as he started paying, it felt like a date and made me worry whether or not I had to kiss him when he dropped me off or accept his calls for dates in the future. Men tend to believe that paying is going to get them in your good graces – hopefully leading to a big fat kiss. I'll tell you what that is: bought affection. I say no thank you! I'd rather pay for my own meal than feel obligated in any way. If you pay for yourself, you're protected and you owe the guy nothing at all. Tell him that if and when you kiss him, thereafter he is invited to pay. Of course, there are always exceptions and being flexible is always as prudent as is being appreciative no matter who pays.

Intelligent Financial Freedom

Once you're out on your own and paying for your own electricity bills, your own dates, and your own shoes to wear on those dates, do NOT mess it up. Don't use the overdraft on your bank account. Don't even bother using credit cards with limits over $1000 because anything above that is terrible to pay off. Have some common sense and only spend the money you have in your bank account.

Besides educational debt and real estate debt, avoid debt like the plague. The Gospel counsels against debt and this applies to everyone. Prophet Ezra Taft Benson discussed the burden and sorrow that debt can cause in his June 1987 Ensign Message; he quotes 2 King's 4:1-7, "Pay thy debt, and live!"[xiv] Consolidate your loans and go to a debt counselor. Find a credit counseling service online. Ask your dad what to do. (Do NOT ask him for money. Have I made that abundantly clear?) Ask your Bishop what to do. No one will laugh at you, but they *will* laugh if you're thirty-five and live at home because you spent all your money highlighting your hair and going to the spa.

Good Girls have self-respect and know how to manage their money. If you aren't rich enough to have an accountant, start gaining control of your finances by going to Budgeting Enrichment meetings, reading about financial independence and following a budgeting chart.

<u>Resources</u>:

- Robin Zenger Baker, "Where Does the Money Go?" Ensign, June 1985. If only I knew, Robin, if only I knew. Oh wait, I do know. The money goes to shoes.

- Janet Thomas, "A Dollar Here, a Dollar There," New Era, Mar. 1990. Practical simple budgeting, for those of us who can barely add.

- Tina Pestalozzi, "Life Skills 101: A Practical Guide to Leaving Home and Living on Your Own." (Did your parents never explain the difference between debit and credit? This book is for you.)

- Students Helping Students, Getting Through College Without Going Broke: A crash course in finding money for college and making it last.

Good Girl Goal #5: Girl's Gotta Work

This is the absolute worst part about preparing to get married. I suffered through it, and so must you. It is absolutely necessary on your path to "marital bliss" because it gives you power. Once you have a real job, nobody can treat you as an inferior. You earn your own money, you pay your own bills, and you are a real adult. This section will walk you through preliminary job searching, specifically how to figure out if your job is temporary or heading toward a career, ten reasons why you should aim for a career, what to look for in a long term job, how to go about landing a job, and some ideas about career areas you might consider.

I Have to Get a Real Job? Boo Hiss Boo!

It sounds overrated, but getting a real job is one of the most rewarding activities of your twenties. I am not talking about a waitressing job. A real job is a job that has direct deposit of your paychecks, regular M-F hours, and a salary if possible. I would like to say that some semi-entrepreneurial or artsy job would count, like being a make-up artist or selling pest control, but sorry, they do not. They are in between jobs for people who don't intend to seriously rely on that occupation. If your job requires regular auditions of any sort, sorry. It's not a real job. If you know how much you make an hour, but not how much you make a year, it probably is not a real job. No more shady jobs for you because you are no longer in high school. The Gap is not a real job, unless you practically run the place. Furthermore, retail jobs make you buy their clothes to work there.

Ten Reasons Why You Should Get a Real Job

1) You get paid regularly.

2) You are entitled to an alluring work wardrobe.

3) Instant worthy nemesis: your boss.

4) You meet interesting people who share your interests.

5) You don't feel lazy.

6) More shoes. Yay!

7) Somewhere to wear new shoes.

8) People think you're responsible.

9) You get experience for your resume and learn valuable skills.

10) You might eventually get to boss someone around.

Position is important as well. It's normal to start on the lowest rung, as an apprentice or trainee. When you're starting out in a new job, be sure to look for the potential to climb the proverbial career ladder. Don't choose a job that doesn't at least have the option to gradually improve your position from apprentice to boss. If extra education will get you a higher position, sign up for the job at trainee level and plan to get the education necessary to advance. Being in charge should be your ultimate goal and a job with some room to grow should require no more than a year of menial labor (making copies, fetching beverages).

The best kind of employment is the type where someone relies on you every day. If nobody relies on you and you could easily skip work without anyone noticing, you need to look for a better job. Having a responsible career improves your self-worth, and that makes you hot. The more responsible you have to be, the more your hotness increases. (Note: Hotness, not haughtiness. Don't be haughty because your important job makes you hot. That will instantly un-hot you).

Ideally, your real job should utilize some part of your brain and challenge you. This is a good thing. Mind you, your job should not be so hard that you find yourself going to work every day when it's dark and coming home when it's dark (unless you live in Iceland and it's winter, in which case, I advise you to move. Brrr!) Long hours are okay, but not as a routine. How will you possibly have time for your many varied hobbies if you work all night? You need to diversify not just your stock portfolio, but also your hours. Doing the same thing all the time makes you really hard to talk to, as you have time for no other interests other than work. Boooorrring!

Using your brain at work is important because it makes each day interesting and different. There are different brain areas: social, analytical, kinesthetic, philosophical, creative, problem solving, etc. If you're really ambitious, chose a career which regularly requires you to use the part of your brain that is lacking. If you'd rather work quietly by yourself, maybe you need a job that forces you to use social skills. Working with the public qualifies as brain work -- the challenge being that every day you have to think of how to avoid maiming others and that improves your social skills.

How a *Good Girl* Lands a Job

Uh, if I knew that, do you think I'd be trying to write church books for a living?

Just kidding. I've had jobs. The following women are good examples of how inexperienced workers find jobs.

Charlotte wanted to be an engineer, but she only had a few years of Community College under her belt. Her classes prevented her from working full time so she took a waitress job at a country club. Though the job paid the bills, Charlotte had to wear comfortable (read: ugly) shoes because she was on her feet all day. Despite the bad shoes, the job situation proved provident for Charlotte because while she was bringing food to rich guys she was able to chat with them and figure out what they did when they weren't hanging about golfing and eating. Charlotte was able to sample the careers of successful people and learned a lot about what type of job she wanted. From one golfer she learned that many civil engineering firms take on young apprentices and then help them pay their way through college. Charlotte kept meeting people and asking them about themselves until one engineer offered her a business card and invited her to come check out the firm. The casual meeting became an interview when Charlotte asked if they had any opportunities for entry level work. She was hired on the spot and with the job came plans to get her through her Bachelor's degree.

Fiona graduated from college and moved to Santa Monica. As soon as she got there, she went to a temp agency without as much as a resume. Fiona didn't know exactly what type of work she wanted to do, but she needed a steady paycheck to pay her rent. At the temp agency she was asked a series of questions about what she was interested in doing and was tested on her office skills. She didn't know how to use a fax machine, but she had a college degree and was willing to learn how to operate office machinery. Within the week, Fiona was filling in for office support staff in an insurance agency. Although Fiona was able to wear fantastic heels because she was sitting down most of the day, she found the work easy and rather boring.

Fiona found herself asking a lot of questions about how the insurance agency is run, and, by the end of the week, she was offered a permanent entry-level position. Insurance was not particularly interesting for Fiona, so she declined; the next week she filled in for an advertising company where she was eventually hired.

Though their interests are different, Charlotte and Fiona have much in common. They both asked questions. Talking to people is the best way to make contact in the working world. Everyone needs to start somewhere and people generally want to help a willing entry level worker get their foot in the door. When it comes to employment, it's really who you know not what you know. Having a college degree shows that you can be taught; many companies are willing to do the teaching if you only ask. Temporary jobs are a great way to experience a variety of work environments.

My dad is the King of the Schmoozers. One of his longest callings for the Church was as Employment Counselor. He gave this advice to new job seekers:

The first thing I'd do when someone came to me looking for a job is send them to the LDS Employment Service Office, which are regionally located. The Employment Office is more for entry-level people who don't have a clue where to begin their job

search, including recent graduates. There's also a Networking Organization Meeting held weekly at the stake center which is aimed more at executives. At the LDS Employment Service Office they help you put together resumes, teach you how to present yourself, and do interviews. I also did some individual coaching on how to make contacts and how to utilize those contacts.

Don't you just love the organization of the church? You have a free employment network at your fingertips. They think of everything. Just ask your Bishop who is in charge of employment in your area and they will be able to set you on the right path.

Another way to get a job is to start out by working for free. Often, people are suspicious of someone who does not require payment for their services, but volunteering is an easy way to make contacts and gain experience. I assume this doesn't work as well in an office environment, but when it comes to working in a hospital, for example, there's always room for a helpful person. You could volunteer in a school, a government organization, a zoo, a theater, or just about anywhere. Most companies have unpaid internships for students who are thinking about going into that field. It needn't be as complicated as a formal internship, you might not get class credit, but volunteering is an easy way in the door for you to experience a potential work environment.

Which Job?

Ever wonder why professional men (such as doctors, dentists, Money-Men, and lawyers) are so universally desired by mothers for their daughters? They require a considerable amount of education and (in a Utopian society) are champions for the people. Americans value professions by the skill required to do the job and their value to society. Doctors have intrinsic value for society, but your mom probably isn't going to shudder if you marry a lawyer. Money-Men (brokers, financial advisers, accountants, etc.) make the world go round. In America, doctors and lawyers have gone to school for longer than most and they have big fat degrees to prove that they are smart. They're so smart that they even put their diplomas on display in their offices so you can be aware of their smartness. Also, they have the financial earning capacity to support a family. Mothers tend to think that this is really important.

But we're not talking about your husband's career, we're talking about yours. You are entitled to be a professional woman, if you choose. There are lots of ways to do this. You can aspire to be a professional in any field in the world. You could go to medical school, law school, or pursue a business degree, a dental certificate, or even a PhD. Or you could work your way into professional companies, put in your time, and end up running the place. Like you, everybody starts at the beginning with careers and nobody knows for sure where life will take them. The way things are looking, you could even be President. If you do become president, I would like some public mention in your acceptance speech. Believe what your teachers told you in grade school: you can be anything you want to be and it's never too late to start.

Job Areas

When choosing your career, remember there are different types of positions in all fields of work. Look on a job search menu to identify what initially looks like just a big amorphous suited world full of suit-wearing business people. Job areas each have their own categories:

Accounting, Finance	Admin/Office Support	Architecture
Engineering	Arts, Media, Design	Biotechnology, Science
Business, Management	Customer Service	Education, Teaching
Government	Human Resources	Internet Engineering
Legal, Paralegal	Marketing, Public Relations	Advertising
Medical, Health	Nonprofit	Retail, Food, Hospitality
Sales, Business Development	Skilled Trade, Craft	Software, Info Technology
TV, Film, Video	Writing, Editing	Choose your own adventure

Bear in mind, however, that the higher the degree you aim for, the more time you're going to have to be in school and paying for school. For example, you could be a doctor. Go to medical school, work really hard and not see the light of day for seven years. There is great need for doctors, of course. People get sick and diseases need cures. Not a bad job but a few drawbacks here: Doctors have horrible hours and their social lives are limited by the demands of their work.

One of my ex-roommates, Eve, was studying to be a doctor. She was very smart, but her studies took up so much of her time that she rarely left the hospital and hardly had time to sleep, let alone attend social activities. Eve was really driven and I admired her work ethic. Her degree took a long time, but when she had finally accomplished her goal she set out to find a husband. By this time, however, Eve looked kind of ragged and worn and was rather out of touch with pop culture and style. Furthermore, she had more education than any man in the Ward other than other doctors, all of whom were pushing thirty with a short stick and also seemed extremely tired. Eve went on to marry one of these doctors and stopped working eventually to have really healthy children. They have doctor friends, but haven't made many friends or participated in many social activities outside of health care. It's one way to live, I guess and this is just one example and of course it's possible to be overworked in any job. Try to not let your personality suffer for the demands of your profession.

The social respect that accompanies being a doctor is also attainable in other professional healthcare careers. Or, you could pursue a career in health services (hospice, nursing, social services, and elder care) that commands similar respect and allows for less school debt and more attractive footwear. By the way, if you work in healthcare, you MUST change your shoes when you get home. White nurse shoes are unacceptable outside of work.

Maybe you could be a lawyer. People may profess not like lawyers, but everybody is glad to know a good one. Lawyers tend to be respected. The ideology of law is appealing, that every one deserves equal treatment under the law, but there are obvious negative associations with lawyers. For some reason public opinion about female lawyers is less scathing than that of their male counterparts. Women lawyers are not considered sharks – it is a perfectly respectable career, and can be extremely lucrative. There are areas in this profession that require less school, for the less ambitious of us. For example, paralegals and legal support do nearly everything a lawyer does but without as much responsibility. Court reporters are high in demand. One drawback of being a lady attorney: you may run into chauvinistic opinion that you are a ball-buster. Go on and bust that myth for us, Gloria Allred.

My friend Theo recently graduated from law school. It's fascinating to hear him talk about the changes that take place in the people who go through such a demanding three years. He knew this one woman, Tamara, who was bubbly and vivacious. She went into law because she wanted to help people and change the world. Having survived three years of law school, Tamara's personality changed enough to be noticeable. She had become more jaded and cynical. Theo says when he met Tamara, he found her caring heart attractive and, as he puts it, "soft." Law school served to rough Tamara up and make her more aggressive, for better or worse. Tamara's experience of law school made her more the stereo-typical aggressive lawyer – maybe she wanted to become so or maybe it just happened. Certainly it's not a woman-only affliction. Either way, it's something to consider. In her defense, Tamara wears great shoes.

Education is the last battlefield of the smart, and it's compensated accordingly. The money is peanuts, but feeling like you're making a difference educating the young minds of America is especially gratifying as you crawl into bed for a nap at three in the afternoon. Fortunately, kids care a lot about shoes and will identify better with you if you wear attractive and current footwear, comfortable or otherwise. The only example you need for considering education as a profession is the thought of that tenured teacher from Middle School who never graded any papers and sat sipping screwdrivers from a Thermos. It's easy to get burnt out.

Whichever career you choose, weigh your options carefully before you get too far along toward your career. Respectable jobs suggest that you are respectable, but basically any career that requires a degree should fit the career expectation and make you more desirable, provided it makes you happy.

Job is a job, right? Well, yes, but your job says certain things about your personality. We can all agree that you are a wonderful person, but if you have a job that reinforces how wonderful you really are, you become all that more attractive. If you've chosen a career that pays you enough to buy shoes, provides you with a challenge, AND demonstrates your innate Christ-like tendencies well then you've scored. Prophet Howard W. Hunter agrees:

Honorable employment is honest employment. Fair value is given and there is no defrauding, cheating, or deceit. Its product or service is of high quality and the employer, customer, client, or patient receives more than he or she expected. Honorable employment is moral. It involves nothing that would undermine public good or morality. For example, it does not involve traffic in liquor, illicit narcotics, or gambling. Honorable employment is useful. It provides goods or services which make the world a better place in which to live. Honorable employment is also remunerative. It provides enough income so that we may be self-sufficient and able to support our families [if necessary,] while leaving us enough time free to be good [mothers] and church workers.[xv]

A little secret regarding jobs: they aren't so awful if you're doing something that improves the world. Unfortunately, most world-improvement jobs make very little cash thereby resulting in fewer shoes. Or worse, the job requires you to wear hiking boots. Nonetheless, if you take one of these jobs you will gain respect and maybe even change your evil shoe coveting ways:

Some Jobs that Help Improve the World

1) Public School Teacher

2) Health Care

3) Social Worker

4) Public Interest Lawyer

5) Red Cross Volunteer

6) The Peace Corps.

7) Postal Service

8) Non-profits

9) Anything to do with Children

10) Elder Care

Be advised, these jobs are generally thankless. I don't think I need to explain the altruism required for such positions; it takes someone near to a Saint to launder soiled linens and run from ferocious dogs, but bad news friend, you're a Latter Day Saint.

1. They look great on a resume.

2. You will go to bed feeling fulfilled.

3. Your future husband will be impressed by your service-minded heart.

I know, I know, its benevolence gone awry to take a job solely on the basis that people will think you are altruistic. But consider: even if you do one of these selfless jobs for your own self gain (like a husband who thinks you're big-hearted) the job is still getting done and you will learn from the experience to be more Christ-like.

Another sad thing about the job situation: you're going to have to work for a while. Change your perspective, ladies. When you take a job, take it with the intention of staying there for many years. There is absolutely no reason for you to assume that you will only need to work for a year or two then get hitched and viola, you get to just raise kids. I know I secretly wished that for myself when I was in college, but the rude wake-up call is just around the corner. You may not find someone worthy of marrying you. You may not have kids. The person you do marry may lose his job. Or, dare I say, you may want to have a career outside of the home for your own self fulfillment.

Chloe followed all the steps. She got a degree and was practicing as a nurse. Chloe landed herself a wonderful husband, Andrew, whom she married in the temple. Within a year or two of marriage they had a delightful little baby (I told you, you get pregnant quickly). Andrew was finishing repaying his army loan for his schooling when he discovered that he would have to go to Iraq for a year. Chloe is an excellent mother and will be while Andrew is gone. She is educated and was self-sufficient before their marriage;

Andrew can rely on her to handle family business in his absence. They will still be getting money from the army enough to live on, but Chloe can go back to work if she chooses. She has an education and work experience. Her family will never go hungry and she has plenty of hobbies to keep her busy while he's away.

Do not shortchange yourself a career – you may have to rely on your work experience in the future. I know we hate to admit it to ourselves, but life throws curve balls and a resume can be your foundation for future employment, as well as a reminder that you can be self-reliant. I often wonder about women in abusive relationships and why they stick around with their loser husbands. Is it because they feel like they could not survive or support their family without the jerk? A career is a form of life-insurance. If you have taught yourself to be self-supporting, your husband will always respect the fact that you can get by without him if he acts up.

Resources:

- "Seven Myths About Careers" by Paul H. Thompson. New Era, January 1985. Interesting article about how some of the working professionals came to find their careers. This is taken from his address at BYU in 1983.

- Yahoo Careers, formally Hotjobs.com

- Recruitment Services, easily found via search engine, some are career specific.

- www.craigslist.org is a great page for all things related to moving, including careers, apartments, moving help, cheap or free furniture, cars etc. Be careful, though, these are strangers. Have someone threatening nearby if you have to meet anyone from the Internet. I've had great success on Craigslist, and you know I check the "missed connections" section, just in case. Side note: I once saw a personal ad for a missed connection that read like this: "Me, SWM, circa 1985, in the middle of a dancing crowd. You, MWF, onstage, pointy bra. You looked right at me; I thought we had a connection. Get in touch." Get it? He was looking for Madonna! Priceless!

- Temp, Staffing, Personnel Agencies. For example, Select Personnel, Officeteam.com, and Kelly. Just do a search on Google; there are 2,850,000 listings at least.

- www.volunteermatch.com

Good Girl Goal #6: Make Yourself Interesting

A major part of maintaining a healthy mental state is having enough to do. When my alarm clock went off every morning at 5:50, the only thing that got me out of bed was the promise that as soon as I got home from work, I could do my hobby. Those hateful steps between your cozy bed and your shower should be time spent thinking about how to spend your free time.

This chapter includes some of my own guilty pleasures starting with some easy hobbies and then moving on to some harder ones. There are a lot of useful ways to spend time, but time does not always need to be used wisely. For some women, the way they waste time ends up being the way they meet their husbands. Time wasting is a misnomer. The activities that are not earning you money are called hobbies.

You've gone to school. You have a job. Don't nobody pay your bills but you. You live somewhere interesting, you're actively working on your testimony. Now what? Take a load off! Go pursue some leisure!

ME Time!

Beatrice has a nine-to-five job as a Human Resources Staffing Manager. She wears heels to work because she doesn't have to stand much.

Beatrice is good at her job and will probably run the place in a few years. On Mondays Beatrice goes to FHE with her ward. On Wednesday she watches reruns of Friends on TBS. On Saturdays, believe it or not, Beatrice hitches free rides on trains.

Being a stowaway is obviously illegal, but Beatrice learned this skill from an experienced hobo friend and is willing to pay fines when she's apprehended. She doesn't really care where the trains take her and she usually gets off the trains less than a few hours away from her destination, although once she did freight hop from Oregon to California with a friend utilizing the symbol communication provided by a network of hitchhikers called the Freight Train Riders of America (or FTRA). Beatrice could be considered a hobo[xvi], but she has a permanent home and only travels on weekends.

I'm not recommending that your hobby needs to be illegal (and admittedly strange) like Beatrice's, but I am suggesting that you pick at least one hobby that makes you unique. Beatrice's inspiration to start being a hobo came from reading work by notable freight-hoppers such as Eugene O'Neill and Jack London. She thought there should be more female vagabonds.

What interests you? What have you always wanted to do, but haven't bothered? There are a million possibilities of things to do with your free time; diversions can be social or religious or lazy or active, just as long as your leisure time makes you happy. Having a variety of hobbies makes you well rounded and interesting.

Ideas for Interesting Spare Time Recreational Pursuits

Beekeeping

Freestyle walking

Visiting Mausoleums

Dumpster Diving

Joining a Scrabble Club

Historical Reenactment (Join the SCA: Society for Creative Anachronism)

Geyser Gazing

Archery

Hang gliding (Beware, lots of people die this way)

Blacksmithing (May cause black lung)

Every single activity that you can think to do has a club somewhere. There are associations for everything. There are people out there who are interested in the same activities you are and they're just waiting to be your friend. Its okay if your hobby is not one of the ones listed above, just as long as you enjoy the activity and it provides a bit of a rest from work. Taking lessons is a great way to get started on your hobby and joining a club is easily achieved by simply checking out your town's community listings. Or you could do an individual hobby. Learn to play an instrument, learn a language, take a stained glass class, teach yourself how to crochet, or make jewelry. If you feel lonely and sad because your husband has not shown up (or reared his head, depending on your perspective) you probably don't have enough to do. Hobbies fill the void that your boyfriend left when you dumped him. If you have time for self pity, you don't have enough hobbies.

Make a list of four things you want to do in your spare time. Begin them right now.

Here is some space for your list:

1)   3)

2)   4)

There are many areas of your brain, and it's doubtful that all of them are accessed at work or school every day. Don't think you have to do a hobby that other people will respect. Just plan to do things that actually sound like a good time for you. The more time you spend doing things that you enjoy, the more you will enjoy your life. School is hard and work can be a drag, even if you have a good job that you like. Fact is, those activities are necessary. The rest of your life is for you to have fun with, so take up some new hobbies. There are things that you look forward to doing as soon as you go off the clock. Expand upon those things. They are your hobbies.

Hobbies can become the reason why you wake up in the morning -- everything else is just leading up to the time when you can do them again. We'll start with the hard hobbies, and then remind you of the easy hobbies in which you probably already participate. The following hobbies will make you feel great for doing them.

Hard Hobbies

1. The dreaded exercise.

It's unbelievably hip to exercise these days. Every gossip magazine has a million photos of perfect bodies emerging sweaty and cheerful from gyms/yoga studios/Pilates classes or what have you. For some odd reason, exercising has become associated with a respectable activity. This is a completely modern development. The world has progressed just fine without regularly scheduled exercise. Winston Churchill was overweight. Pavarotti is big. Queen Latifa is no size 2. Remember that fertility statue, the Venus of Willendorf? Squatty and round.

I am not advocating an unhealthy lifestyle. Notice how eating is not included as a hobby. Everybody requires exercise to keep us healthy; many of us require extra regular exercise to combat bad genes. However, exercise should not rule your life. Having a healthy lifestyle does not include a daily dose of self-hatred that fuels a lot of workouts. Balance is more important than the weight your scale reports. They say you get your endorphins going when you exercise and you feel really good after you get your heart rate up. This may be true, but I often wonder if the improved, energized mood isn't just your brain telling you, "Good job for working out. You can feel like less of a sloth for the rest of the day." If you can pick a few days out of the week to be happy in your own skin, then you don't need the post-workout endorphin surge.

Exercise and dieting can easily become an addiction. As in the other areas of our lives, the Prophet Joseph F. Smith counseled, "The Saints should not be unwise, but rather understand what the will of the Lord is, and practice moderation in all things."[xvii] The problem with exercise and dieting is that during your twenties, people will look for any excuse to explain why they're unhappy or even why they're unmarried. Size does not matter for finding a husband, but being the best you can be does. These go hand in hand. The way you feel about your body is individually determined and most young women have to be taught to love their bodies. The external pressure to lose weight and loathe the way you look is a lot to bear. Every body has its own happy weight and that is all we should try to accomplish. Oprah will never be a size two. You must not let your body affect the way you feel about yourself.

Dazzling Famous Women Who Are Not Tiny:

Oprah. (No matter her weight)

Marilyn Monroe

Beyonce

Drew Barrymore

Kate Winslet

Scarlett Johansson

Toni Colette

Queen Latifa

Getting married does not require dropping a dress size. They make temple clothes in convenient drape-like cuts. Around the world every different size and shape of body is valued for different reasons. All right, so you have big momma hips. Maybe the last time you were anything less than a size ten was when you were ten years old. Doesn't matter. You don't have to be in shape at all to get married, but you do need to dress appropriately for your body. When the scriptures say "be ye therefore perfect" they're not talking about your body, they're talking about discipline. Take a hint from the scriptures; it's my favorite gospel loop-hole. You can't be perfect by yourself; you have to be perfected in Christ.

Here's how it applies to exercise: All you have to do is TRY.

Trying includes putting on your work-out clothes. Trying includes running around your block. Fifteen minutes of trying to exercise per day actually works to strengthen and tone. I recently learned that running around the block by my house (okay, mostly walking) counts as exercise. Don't be so hard on yourself about this one. It's great if you find something exercisy that you enjoy, but if you loathe everything that involves breaking a sweat (like I do) just put on some exercise clothes and count yourself halfway there. We're not aiming for absolute perfection in this book. We just want people to think you're trying.

Putting the word 'exercise' on your to do list is just vague enough. Cross it out when you have run up and down the stairs three times because you kept forgetting things. Cross it out when you carry all your groceries home without a shopping cart. Exercising is personally determined and subjective. When people ask you if you exercise, say yes. Then even if you're overweight, they'll respect you for trying to get in shape.

Read a different book if you want to go the whole hog. I say fake it until you make it.

The best way to fake exercise is simply by wearing exercise clothes. Buy some! That's completely justifiable shopping! Make them cute so you'll want to put them on, even better if somebody "catches" you in your work-out clothes. Then you get extra points: not only are you adorable, you're trying to get in shape. Presentation is everything; don't feel guilt about allowing people to think you have discipline. Maybe you'll be inspired to actually break a sweat. Plus, it's really fun to tell people you have to take a nap because you're so tired from exercising.

Extra bonus: work-out wear doubles as really comfy pajamas.

2. Reading.

Reading makes you smarter. Vocabularies are reflective of literature, and literature is considered to be written works of artistic merit. Loop-hole! Art is in the eye of the beholder. Therefore, US Weekly and *The Nanny Diaries* are technically literature! Reading is a fun hobby and generally respected, provided that you can throw in a classic every now and then. Granted, if you're following the words of the Prophet, you are reading a classic every day. We call them scriptures. Round out your hobbies with religious and secular reading, even if it's just old Calvin and Hobbes. Benefits of reading: Puts you right to sleep, appropriate for nap time and night time, entertaining when eating alone, and even makes you feel like you're eating alone on purpose. My mother keeps a book with her at all times so that she's never bored. Also, she looks smart. Here's a little trick I learned from my bishop – cover the books you're embarrassed of reading with the book jacket from something classic that you've already read.

My Bishop once told me to read *The Miracle of Forgiveness* by Spencer W. Kimball. I told him that everyone would laugh at me because I was a big fat sinner and I left the copy in his office. The following day, he dropped off a package at my house. Inside was *The Miracle of Forgiveness* covered in a homemade book jacket. The title on the front was *Crime and Punishment*. Never judge a book by its cover, right? Nobody asked any questions and I like to believe they thought I was smart and not a sinner. Good book. Love that Dostoevsky.

3. Church Things.

It goes without saying that participation in the gospel is the single most valuable thing you do with your time. Elder NAM said, "If you have not chosen the kingdom of God first, it will, in the end, make no difference what you have chosen instead." This is a subtext for this book, and if you're reading it, your testimony of and desire for a temple marriage is implicit. Therefore, we will skip a Sunday School lesson on why church is important and move right on into how church participation will help you towards your righteous goal.

Why doesn't anybody ever mention how difficult it is to do everything that is expected of a lovely LDS lass? Participating in church is not a hobby, it's a lifestyle and anyone who tells you being a member of the church is easy is selling something. It's not easy, but it's worth it, as they say. Participating in church activities takes up a lot of time and acts as a great social vehicle. You can pretty much guarantee that if it's a church sponsored activity there will be something rewarding involved, such as a lesson or service project or physical activity. That's all well and good, but when you're single, all of these church activities double as thinly disguised dating rituals. That Singles Wards exist at all is a testament to the fact that the gospel encourages making families. Thus, we should take advantage of as many church sponsored matching meetings as possible. Go on telling yourself you're going to play soccer with a bunch of veritable strangers because you like it. You aren't. I'm willing to bet you quit playing intramural soccer as soon as you get married.

Making church activity (beyond that which is expected on Sundays) part of your lifestyle could potentially take up all your free time, as the Lord's work is never done. The Lord's work for you at this time in your life is, as Hinckley said, for you to create eternal families. That Singles activities are meat markets is just part of the package. Landing a spouse can be extremely trying but we all must suffer through it.

Be thankful that your Single's Ward leaders think up ways to improve your life and feel free to show up to as many activities as you can. Being a patron and a support of church activity is a form of a calling because somebody spends their time planning lessons, activities and social events for you. It's classy to support their effort. Say you're going to support, leave with a spouse. You may hate going to church dances, doing service, and going to firesides. Deal with it; there is much to gain by being in the right place at the right time. Church activities are always the right place to be.

4. Doing nice things for others.

A great way to occupy your time is to find a charitable organization or opportunity and join up. Even if it's just for one hour once a week, the benefits are immeasurable. Yet, I will measure them for you:

Makes others feel good.

Makes you feel good.

Makes the world a better place.

P.S., It's a commandment.

You may not be surprised to learn that I believe charity is subjective as well. You can do easy charity or you can do hard charity, doesn't matter which 'cause "Charity never faileth." Church callings do not really fall under the explicit category of charity because they are your job for the Lord and you're already expected to do your calling. You could expand upon your calling, having already magnified it. You could do something not even involved in your calling, just because you see a job that you could do voluntarily. Responsibility means seeing a job that needs doing and doing it without being asked. This is also charity.

Here is a list of ideas for charity. Do one a week if you want charity light. Do one a day if you need a daily dose of goodness:

Easy Charity

1.   Call your grandmother.

2.   Pick up trash in your exercise clothes (two birds, one stone)

3.   Volunteer somewhere you like to be.

4.   Give someone a make-over.

5.   Write a nice note.

6.   Invite an acquaintance to lunch.

7.   Hold a door open for somebody.

Of course, you could go the extra mile and actually get involved in an organized charity. In 1989, GBH's address to single sisters recalled the services of Florence Nightingale and Clara Burton, inviting single women to find themselves by giving their time:

> **There are so many out there whose burdens you can lift. There are the homeless, there are the hungry, there are the destitute all around us. There are the aged who are alone in rest homes. There are handicapped children, and youth on drugs, and the sick and the homebound who cry out for a kind word. If you do not do it, who will?[xviii]**

You're out there looking for somebody to love, but why limit yourself to romantic love? You have the time because you aren't tied to making dinner for a man and his offspring. Why not take the focus off yourself for a few hours a week and quit worrying about finding a husband? The Prophet sees service as a cure-all: "The best antidote I know for worry is work. The best medicine for despair is service. The best cure for weariness is the challenge of helping someone who is even more tired."[xix]

The most rewarding kind of hobbies to pursue include getting more education or volunteering for something that will look good on your resume. Working for free is a great way to burrow into jobs in which you have little or no experience; volunteering is a great way to give back to the community while at the same time improving your self worth. Church work might be considered a hobby, but really, it's the Lord's work and you're required to do it. Exercising, reading, doing church work and doing nice things for others are a few among many productive hobbies. We've discussed these hobbies that will actually improve your life. Do one of these hard hobbies, then follow it with an easy hobby chaser. Easy hobbies will not look good on your resume. The easy hobbies won't help you get a job or find your true love, unless your true love appreciates the easy hobbies as much as you do. Nonetheless, these activities have served to keep me busy. Feel free to try some of them.

Low Commitment Hobbies

1. Napping.

Feel no guilt about taking naps. Many people talk down about naps. Don't listen to those people. It is perfectly acceptable to take a nap every day because it's good for you. A brother from my ward once said, "If you want to do something good for an hour, take a nap. If you want to something good for more than an hour, do something charitable for someone else." Naps cannot be your only hobby (no Rip van Winkles) but in moderation they'll do you good. A 2003 Harvard University study shows that Aa 60- to 90-minute siesta can charge up the brain's batteries as much as eight hours tucked up in bed."[xx] If you're well rested, you will be more likely to be your best self. Here are some people who advocate naps, feel free to note them to anti-nap people: Winston Churchill, Albert Einstein, John F. Kennedy, Lyndon B. Johnson, Thomas Edison, Napoleon Bonaparte, Lenore Craven, Johannes Brahms, Ronald Reagan, Leonardo Da Vinci, John D. Rockefeller, Eleanor Roosevelt, William J. Clinton, and Gene Autry.

2. Shopping.

I would really like to be able to tell you that I use all my spare time to help feed hungry people and care for the sick. I imagine I would happier if I spent my time that way, but realistically every free moment you have is not going to be dedicated to charity. I'm really sorry to have to tell you this, but I love to shop. It is useless, materialistic and is not a priority in my life (beyond food shopping), but it is one of my hobbies. I'm not advocating buying useless things. There are definitely better things to do with your time then shop, but there is a place for shopping in the life of a woman who wants to get married. Notice that I didn't write 'buy things' I wrote 'shop.' You don't have to buy anything at all to shop. You can shop at high end places or at a drug store. They are equally satisfying.

If you're going to have a shopping hobby, cultivate it and do it right. See how many stores you can go in and find something you have to have and then leave without buying it. Watch fifteen things on e-bay and don't bid on a single one. Court items but control your buying. The best shoppers are not the ones who buy the best things, they're the people who only buy what they want and get incredible deals. Furthermore, just about everybody shops. You do need shoes to wear. It's okay if your hobby involves finding the perfect pair for the lowest price. Maybe my hobby isn't really shopping, it's bargain hunting. That sounds better. Check yourself so that shopping doesn't translate to blatant materialism and greed. I'll try to do the same.

Furthermore, shopping has direct applications to preparing yourself for marriage. Shopping does play a part in presenting the best product for getting married. That will be covered in the "Get Gorgeous, Girl!" section.

3. Watching TV.

Oddly enough, television has become so much a part of our society that it seems like a real hobby. Remember, we're still in the easy hobby section. Watching TV is not going to make you a better person. However, it is going to give you something to talk about with people with whom you might otherwise have nothing in common. TV shows and movies are excellent water cooler fodder. Popular culture has become a social activity. I'm not a regular TV watcher and I grew up without cable. When I bought my first TV, I threw an "I Bought a TV" party and had a group of eligible people over to watch a movie. I'm still friends with a number of them. You may have no interest or idea about the latest Friends-type show on TV (be careful that the shows meet an acceptable rating standard), but you may be considered a social pariah if you can't chime in every once in a while. You don't have to watch them all, but if you pick a popular one or a sport, it's become a social activity to watch an admittedly stupid show in a group on a weekly basis. My friend Allison has sat through about twenty episodes of Orange Country or County or whatever it's called just because she met new people every time she went to the weekly Orange County airing at a friend's house. She hates that show, but it's a good place to meet people.

All right, those are the easy hobbies and that's all I'm going to say about them because, let's be honest, they're not great uses of time. Easy hobbies are meant to help you unwind and relax. If you've had your fill of napping, shopping and watching TV, you might investigate resources for hobby development such as the Internet and local community centers. Having hobbies is an easy way to make friends and make you more interesting for the men-folk.

Doing things for your own improvement can also benefits humanity. Do the world a favor – take a shower and brush your hair. Get a make-over for yourself. Paired with real service, self improvement makes you happy. Together, they make the world a better place.

Resources:

- www.timeout.com. "Your guide to a good time." Online magazine for nearly every major metropolitan area. Great for local restaurants, theater, events, concerts, community activities.
- The United Nation's Volunteers Program is easily accessed at www.unv.com
- www.ldsevents.com. LDS Living Magazine has listings of pageants and church events going on all over the place.
- Sark, *Change Your Life Without Getting Out of Bed*. The ultimate nap book.
- The Complete Idiot's Guide Series. Terrible title, fun books to introduce you to any topic you want to learn.

- Edythe K. Watson, "Crochet a Rope of Pearls," Ensign, Nov. 1971, 75. Directions for Crocheting a rope of pearls. Bit of a strange hobby.

- Solveig Paulson Russell, "Deltiology," Friend, July 1981, 33. Deltiology means collecting postcards.

- Doing your Family History is a great hobby. Ask your Family History Leader at your ward how to get started.

Good Girl Goal #7: I'm Enduring, so now what?

Josephine is a charming capable woman. She's twenty-six years old and she has a fulltime job working for the Humanities Department at a prestigious college. Josephine has been on her own since age nineteen when she began college, with only minor help from her parents. After college Josephine worked for three years and saved to go back to school so that she could get her Master's degree. Josephine has a strong testimony and is very active in church. She plays the violin and visits with her family regularly. She's so busy you practically have to corner her to get her to rest and go out to dinner during the week. Josephine is elegant and has a covetable array of shoes in her closet, including some sensational five-inch black patent leather peep-toes. She gets asked out frequently by guys in her single's ward and she has boyfriends now and again. Her husband has not shown up yet, but she hasn't had time to even notice or worry about finding the right guy. Josephine plays it cool, but unfortunately, she's just not very happy.

This is a common plague for single LDS men and women. They get disenchanted with the world and feel that although they're very busy, life just isn't very exciting right now. Josephine has everything any girl would want but she feels bored and apathetic. This section is devoted to finding ways to be happy and motivated while you're waiting to take the next step in your eternal progression. You'll be introduced to the *Good Girl's Happy Triangle* and get some suggestions for things (other than marriage) to look forward to.

Being educated, busy, and self sufficient empowers women with confidence. Paired with the gospel, we have every reason to be satisfied and happy with our lives. Despite the "good news" of the gospel, many young women suffer melancholy and frustration because they are thus far unable to achieve their goal of being married for eternity. Even though Josephine's life seems picture perfect to everyone else, she still feels like she's just killing time until the next stage in her life.

Yep, you're killing time. You really are. Between Young Women's and marriage there doesn't seem to be much to stimulate your emotions. Education is satisfying. Having a job is rewarding. Hobbies are entertaining. But how do you stay happy while you're checking off items on your personal to-do list?

What Josephine needs is *"The Good Girl's Happy Pyramid"*. In order to be happy while you endure, you need these three things:

"The *Good Girl's* Happy Pyramid"

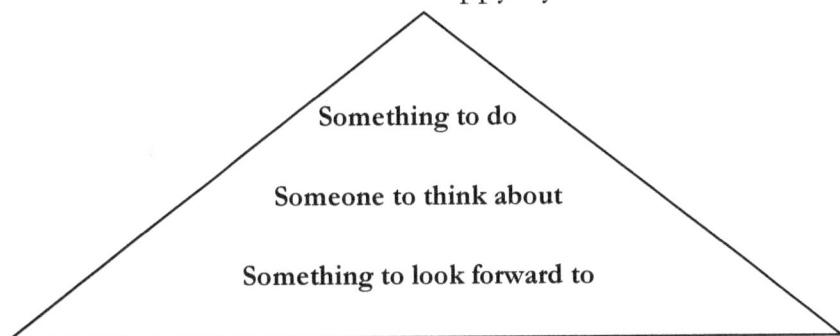

Something to do

Someone to think about

Something to look forward to

Now, if you've been following the *Good Girl Goals*, you've got more than enough to do (getting an education, working toward a career, doing your hobbies, etc.). If you don't have anything to do, return to page one and re-read this book. That ought to kill at least, what, seventeen minutes? Because you're so busy, accomplished and charming, men will float in and out of your life and they will give you plenty to think about. If you're actively looking for a husband (as outlined in the Delightful Dating section to follow) then you'll be picking through the men faster than it takes me to pick out and eat all the chocolate chips out of a Mrs. Field's cookie. Thinking about lots of men is one of the highlights of being single. After you get married, you only get to think about one man (unless he's schizophrenic). Josephine might have lots to do and a bevy of men to think about, but she isn't happy because she doesn't have something specific to look forward to.

Something to Look Forward To

Josephine has tons of things to do. She has work, she has hobbies and family, she has friends to hang with and books to read. Nearly every minute of Josephine's day is filled with something useful or fun, she's serving in church or she's socializing with friends. Josephine usually has a boyfriend, but when she doesn't she has at least one or two prospects who interest her. However, Josephine does not have anything specific to anticipate.

Looking forward to an event or activity in the future is an art form. There are the regular markers throughout the year such as birthdays, holidays, and sick days but having a special and unique event that is a definite thing to look forward to will keep your life stimulating. The length of time to anticipate the affair must be at least a few months away, but within a reasonable time frame so that you can still be excited. A little less than a year is long enough to wait for your goal.

The most obvious thing that people look forward to is a vacation. A vacation is an excellent year long-term goal. Other long-term goals could be something less dramatic, like buying an item you really want and have to save for. It's basically the idea that you're making yourself a little promise of a reward so that life feels like there's a light at the end of the tunnel.

We are conditioned to section off segments of the year. It's impossible to reach June and not secretly think to yourself "School's out for the summer!"

Why, in our adult lives, do we abandon that big carrot dangling just out of reach? I say, reinstate the carrot! I need some regular motivation and if work ain't gonna set me loose come June, I'm gonna invent something great to look forward to! Here are some ideas:

Can Hardly Wait!

A trip to Hawaii or another exotic beach.

A puppy.

The diamond ring you secretly want (Right hand rings are so "In")

A new job.

A new apartment

A new car

Going back to school

A luxurious spa weekend, with massage and facial

Christian Louboutin heels

Attending an open house of a new temple

A nice piece of furniture

A cruise

Tickets to a show or concert

Now, I'm not advocating saving money and then blowing it on something worthless and trivial. If you plan far ahead, you can budget for a reward as well as put some cash in a safety savings account. Working hard should have rewards other than simply making ends meet. Improve your quality of life by planning for something you have always wanted and go out and get it! If it's a strand of pearls, opera tickets or a week of reading trashy novels in your room, prepare for it and set a date. Planning for things is hard work and waiting is even harder! You can justify your completely self-indulgent prize or activity by calling it "patience training." Having patience and enduring to the end is absolutely a gospel principle, First Nephi blares it loud and clear, "and if they endure unto the end they shall be lifted up at the last day, and shall be saved in the everlasting kingdom of the Lamb."[xxi]

Well, enduring to the end in the gospel is going to be hard, right? Maybe we should practice our enduring until we reach the final goal. Learning patience in an unconventional way is still learning patience, and you still get a prize at the end. Who says the reward at 'the end' isn't the long awaited annual Macy's Labor Day sale? If I endure my way to the end and make it to heaven, you better believe my heaven's going to have shoe closets that will make Imelda Marcos blush. However, if you're less materialistic than I am, traveling is always a satisfying and worthy reward for hard work.

See the World!

Some of the greatest things about being in your twenties are the massive discounts on travel opportunities. Student-age people (and young professionals) are encouraged to travel abroad by offers applicable only to those under thirty. International Student Identity Cards (ISIC) are available to students under twenty-six and the International Youth Travel Card is great for under twenty-six non-students, both available on the ISIC webpage along with a variety of discount offers. Student Travel Association (STA) is a great resource all around the world for student travel recommendations, support and deals as well as enticing opportunities for studying, working, and volunteering abroad. One of STA's newer programs offers language courses in thirty different countries. How fun does that sound? Eurail passes for trains all over Europe are discounted for travelers under twenty-six. Notice a pattern? Being twenty-six must mean that you're really an adult and are expected to pay full fare. Personally, I'm not happy about learning that little age tidbit, but you should definitely reap the benefits while they're out there.

Before I was married I studied Shakespeare for a summer in London, rode an elephant in Thailand, rappelled down a two hundred foot cliff, munched on tapas in Barcelona, drove the car I bought with my own money down the Mexico coast, winked at lifeguards in Hawaii, and slept in an ice cave.

Those were only a handful of my pre-martial adventures, and I look forward to sharing just as many with my spouse in the years to come.

Here's some space for your own personal list of adventures to take.

Things I Want to Do Before I Get Hitched

1)	2)
3)	4)
5)	6)

Of course, you don't have to just go places that are outside of the US, but traveling internationally is an excellent way to broaden your horizons and learn about other cultures. There are so many beautiful places HF created for you, why not get out there and check 'em out? Travel creates lasting memories, and who knows? Maybe your husband lives in Australia and he's just waiting for you to come fall in love with him. Planning that once-in-a-lifetime trip is a great thing to look forward to. There are coconuts to drink from, elephants to ride, and crepes to eat! If you've never ridden in a jeepney, snacked on wurst in Prague, or flipped a penny into the Trevi fountain, then, girl, you need to buy a guide book, pack a suitcase and pick a day to set off on a trip to see the world!

Resources:

- www.statravel.com

- www.travelocity.com almost always the cheapest for flights.

- www.isic.com

- Let's Go Guidebooks to whatever country you want to visit – they're for a younger traveler

- Any travel book by Rick Steves. This man is a travel guru and he makes great recommendations for food, transportation, and lodging.

- www.travel.state.gov This site is where you can begin your passport application and it also has information about Visas, which are generally only required for a stay of over six weeks.

- Also check out a local University's Study Abroad office.

Good Girl Goal #8: Securing Your Testimony

While you're covering the basics of adult living, you're going to be continually polishing and refining your testimony. The beginning of your adulthood is when you lay the groundwork for the rest of your life. You probably promised your Beehive leader that you were going to get married in the temple, but now you need to revisit that promise and create a plan to achieve that goal. One of the most startling things I learned about my peers during my time as an unmarried LDS young adult is that **many, many people struggle with their testimonies**. The years between eighteen and twenty-one are the foundation of your adulthood, and also some of the most formative. The way you spend these years can make or break the rest of your life. In this chapter, we're going to reflect on testimonies, discuss some of the lies Satan concocts to dissuade young adults from righteous living, and talk about the blessings of repentance.

The Conversion Continuum

There is no such thing as an unchanging testimony of the gospel. I believe that everyone who is an active member of the LDS church experiences conversion and that the process of conversion is continual throughout our lives. Everyone encounters peaks and valleys with their testimony whether publicly or privately. This is a good thing! Heavenly Father doesn't just care that our names are on the books, He tests us daily, year in and year out to see where we are with our belief in the gospel and our reliance on Him. That's why they call membership in the Church "activity" – because we're all actively trying to align our wills to the way of the Father. It's an active process and one that is often painful and hard.

One thing young women frequently forget is that HF wants you to make it to the Celestial Kingdom. He's counting on you! You are in control of whether you get there or not. It's called **free** agency for a reason – you're free to choose eternal life. Come on, is there really any other *reasonable* alternative?

Despite our best efforts to believe and practice the gospel, sometimes we're led astray. Being led astray can be a state of mind as much as it can be a lifestyle. Many young adults live with massive feelings of inadequacy, guilt and self doubt. Some think that they do not deserve the happiness provided by temple marriage and so they stop communicating with HF. Everyone deserves to be happy, and the gospel provides a path toward happiness. I've compiled a list of self-destructive and counterproductive thoughts and attitudes I've witnessed among my Sisters in the gospel in order to help you wade through the lies.

Big Fat Lies Satan Tells Young People (and their Debunking)

1. You don't think you deserve to be married in the temple.

Wrong! Everyone is part of a family and deserves to be sealed to them for eternity. HF wants you to create your own eternal family by going to the temple, and He has provided a way to do so. No matter what you've done, you can make it right through repentance. Do you believe that the words of all the prophets don't apply to you? If you repent, you can be clean and be one more step on your way to returning to live with HF. Don't cheat yourself. Temple marriage is always within your grasp if you want it to be.

2. You feel too embarrassed to repent.

Uh, Christ has heard it all before. Your Bishop has probably heard most of it before. Think your sin is original? Did you spray paint your neighbor's house on a Sunday while eating excessive amounts of red meat? I don't think so. Christ has seen it all before. Try checking those books, what are they called? Oh yeah, the Scriptures. Example upon example of people making bad choices, falling away, and turning back to the gospel. Check out Saul, Alma the younger, Alma the Priest of King Noah, Korihor (they called this guy an anti-Christ, you're not even close to that bad), and others during Christ's ministry (you find it in the New Testament).

3. You keep repeating the same sin, God won't forgive you again.

Yes, He will. We learn lessons little by little. If you let the sin that plagues you win, Satan has won and that is no good. The first step to recovery is admitting you have a problem. Your Bishop can show you how to get help if you need it.

4. You don't feel bad about your sins.

Hey, it happens. We tell ourselves any sort of lie in order to make sin more palatable. The first time it may be great, but eventually sin wears us down to the point of numbness. Sin always catches up to you, but sometimes you get so far in that you don't really care anymore. Here's the interesting part: you have the gift of the Holy Ghost and you will be blessed with discord in your life if you're living sinfully. HF will help you feel remorse if you are living sinfully. Even if you're not ready to repent, you can still open the line of communication between you and HF by saying a prayer and telling Him how you feel. Showing just that little bit of faith helps. Pray to feel remorse for your shortcomings and for the desire to repent.

5. You feel like you failed at being a church member and have decided to "move on".

Sorry, but once you've experienced the Holy Ghost and have ever had the confirmation that the gospel is true, you can't just quit! The gospel is the truth, and if you've ever felt a confirmation from the spirit, the gospel will always be part of your psyche. If it's been a while since you've felt the peace of truth and you feel like you're alone, try praying and telling HF what's going on with you.

Try going to church, meet with the missionaries, and talk to your bishop. Less publicly, read your favorite scripture, listen to the hymn you remember you loved, or just say a little prayer. Heavenly Father's out there, He loves you, and He wants you to have all the blessings in the world. Comfort and companionship are available if you only ask, no matter who you are or how bad things get.

6. You shouldn't care about your eternal salvation right now.

Why not? The gospel is the one guaranteed resource of peace and happiness. Even if you're not ready to get married, you can still work on your own testimony and fill up your spirituality well for times of trouble. Making effort has got to count for something in the gospel and even if you feel like you're just going through the motions at church, they are still good habits. If you can't drum up the interest and feel like quitting church, try making a list of gospel things that are easy for you and things that are hard. Do the easy ones, say a prayer and tell HF that you're working on the hard ones, and then work on them. You don't have to be perfect, you just have to try.

7. You think all other church members are lemmings.

The gospel is perfect, the people are not. Everyone is at a different place in the gospel and you have no idea what problems they face in their personal lives. They may all look perfect and ready for translation up to heaven but remember that they are human and life is hard for everyone in different ways. Besides, church isn't about whoever's there – it's about you and you following the commandments. I don't care if everyone is a cyborg replica, you aren't and you need to be as active as possible. Furthermore, if all other church members look and act exactly the same, then you need to be there as an example for other people who feel the same way you do (you can come sit by me!). If you're the only person of your race, style, or type, then good for you. The gospel takes all kinds. Go and mix things up. Growing up, my husband was the only Asian in his ward. When non-white people visited, I don't doubt that they were glad to see him there.

8. God doesn't answer your prayers, so you quit talking to Him.

I fall into this one all the time. I like giving HF the silent treatment if I don't get what I want. When you have specific desires, it's hard to learn the will of the Father. But we have to have faith that God answers prayers. Have you prayed for anything, ever? Have you ever had a prayer answered? Yes, you have. Heavenly Father answers prayers, even if He does so in His own inexplicable way. When you get bogged down in this one, pray that you might know what HF wants from you and pray that you'll be happy doing His will. You can look for me in the afterlife asking HF about all my strangely answered prayers. We're going to have a long chat.

9. It's been so long since you've been to church it would be too weird to go back.

One of the places you are always welcome is at church. It may feel weird going to church again, but everyone starts somewhere. Most of us have missed church every now and again for one reason or another and felt that uncomfortable feeling of going back. It takes a lot of humble character to get back in the game, but it's worth it. Trying is the most important thing; the greatest journey starts with the first step. If you must work your way in, try going to another ward. Or, just stay as long as you feel comfortable. The gospel is all about commitment, but nowhere is it written that you can't take this at your own pace. The end goal is salvation, but we have our whole lives to learn how to be perfect.

10. People will judge you.

My mother likes to tell me "nobody notices, nobody cares." She's partially right, but really, "most people don't notice, most people don't care." Maybe some people will judge you, but everybody has been through repentance and knows how hard it can be. Technically, they're breaking a commandment by judging you. Shrug them off. This is about you and the Lord.

All of these lies we tell ourselves are courtesy of Satan – they've got his name written all over them. The devil's main goal is to make us believe that the gospel is not for us. He's crafty, that Satan. Crafty in a bad way.

Where There's a Will, There's a Way

If you can identify whatever's keeping you from full temple worthy membership in the gospel as one of Satan's tricks, then you're a step ahead.

Many of my closest friends have felt defeated and unhappy because they've started to believe the lies that Satan has told them.

Ebony was raised in the gospel and was the second daughter in a righteous LDS family. During high school, Ebony got involved with the wrong crowd and started doing drugs regularly. She quit going to church when she was about sixteen. Ebony has had a series of boyfriends, some of whom have lived with her. She quit living the Word of Wisdom years ago. Ebony doesn't own her own scriptures anymore and generally does not lead an LDS lifestyle, though she does attend all family related church activities and maintains a fairly good relationship with her brother and sisters.

Recently I had dinner with Ebony and she was telling me about her boyfriend, Wes. Wes isn't a member of the church and they've been dating for two years. Ebony told me she's anxious to get married, but she's concerned because Wes isn't LDS. Wes frequently asks Ebony if she's ready to get engaged, but Ebony finds her religious conflict too difficult to talk about with Wes because she fears it will drive them apart. Ebony hasn't been an active member for whatever reason, but she still knows about temple marriage and believes that it's important.

The possibility of marriage has caused Ebony to face her testimony. She worries that if she gets married outside of the temple her family won't support her, but she's been living with Wes and not living an LDS lifestyle. Ebony's beliefs conflict with her way of life. Currently, she's been thinking about introducing Wes to the gospel, but even doing that is scary because she's going to have to explain to Wes why she wasn't living an LDS life if she really believed in it.

Love frequently presents these sorts of problems. Ebony and Wes may seem ill-fated, but they are just as deserving of happiness as any of us. They will have to make some serious changes in their lives if they want to marry in the temple, but it is not an impossibility. Of course we want to share the gospel with the people that we love, but if we've been living unrighteous lives we are met with a great challenge: conversion. Conversion doesn't just mean believing, it means aligning your life choices to reflect your beliefs. Ebony can get back on the path toward temple marriage and HF will help her, whether she ends up with Wes or not.

Repentance

Unfortunately, most of us stumble a lot along life's path and feel like we're so marred by our decisions that we somehow have lost the privilege of complete repentance. When a church member makes a poor choice, they sin knowingly and even know the consequences of that sin. This is what makes repentance so difficult – we knew our sin was wrong before we did it, and yet still we went ahead and committed the sin. Logically, that's just stupid. Ridiculous though it may be, we all do this all the time. Everyone, including the General Authorities of the church, has made mistakes. Everyone, save Christ, has sinned despite knowing the error of their choice. Thankfully, the Atonement applies to everybody, no matter what kind of mess you made.

The Atonement applies to everyone, all the time. Heavenly Father is merciful and Jesus Christ has seen it all before. They will understand. When I've made horrendous choices, I've prayed for the desire to stop making those choices. I like to think that even my little prayers asking for help to turn from my sinful ways are a way of raising a white flag. Prayers begging for the desire to believe show a modicum of faith. It is impossible to lead a sinless life – everyone is somewhere on the continuum of sin and repentance. If you have faith enough to tell HF what's going on with you and ask for a little help, He will have mercy on you. Prayers are private so pray for what you need (at whatever volume. He'll still love you if you need to shout).

No matter what you did, Heavenly Father can forgive you. Even if you're weak and repeat the same mistake, Heavenly Father can forgive you. (Are you seeing a merciful pattern developing here?) Even if you're horribly embarrassed of the thing you did, Heavenly Father can forgive you and you can be clean again. Consider the scripture, "Come now, and let us reason together, saith the Lord: though your sins be as scarlet, they shall be as white as snow; though they be red like crimson, they shall be as wool" (Isaiah 1:18).

I love the part where Isaiah says "let us reason together, saith the Lord" because it seems so unreasonable to most of us – that our horribly embarrassing sins could become clear and white. But if the Lord says so, who are we to doubt that our sins can be made white as snow? Learning to believe that we're really forgiven in our sinful state is essential to our spiritual freedom and happiness in the gospel. For the best treatment of this subject, read *Believing Christ*. It's an approachable manual to personal application and understanding of the Atonement. That book really helps my testimony.

Once you understand and apply the Atonement in your life by repenting, the next step is learning to see yourself as HF does. Even if you are a big sinner, HF does not label you that way and give up on you. You are not a lost cause, so quit acting like one. There is always, always a path back to all the great things in the gospel. Our pride often inhibits us from admitting our mistakes, but that is just a tool of the lying ol' Devil. It takes courage to admit our weakness – courage and meekness. Good news! Meek people inherit.

One last thing: our spirituality is between us and Heavenly Father. Your sins are private and people don't need to know unless they're directly involved. Save yourself humiliation by keeping mum about your problems because they don't need to be broadcast. If you learn about another person's sins, don't go telling other people even if you think it's for a good reason. There is no good reason to talk about other people's problems outside of their company. We're all in this thing together. In the words of the artist formally known as the artist formally known as Prince: "Dearly beloved, we are here to get through this thing called Life."

Resources:

- Stephen E. Robinson, "Believing Christ".

- Sheri L. Dew, "No One Can Take Your Place".

- Bruce C. Hafen, "The Broken Heart".

- Talk to Heavenly Father. Pray.

- Read the words of the Prophets in conference talks available at www.lds.org

- Listen to Build Me Up, Buttercup by the Foundations. It is impossible to feel sad when you listen to that song. Also, for good measure Prince's Let's Go Crazy.

- Meet with your Bishop, possibly find an LDS therapist

- Search, ponder, and read the Scriptures. Make it a habit; it will become the rock of your testimony.

Good Girl Goal #9: Making the Mission Decision

Claire wanted to serve a mission. She was extremely faithful and prepared diligently to serve the Lord. It wasn't easy for Claire to prepare for a mission. She had just finished college and had to save up enough money to go, but she prayed about her decision and felt that it was the right opportunity. As soon as Claire turned twenty-one, she completed her paperwork and excitedly awaited her call to serve. Finally, the letter came in the mail. Claire was thrilled to be called to Italy and couldn't wait to learn the language. While she was waiting for the first of March, the day for her to report to the MTC, Claire radiated excitement and joy. It was this joy, in fact, that attracted Tobias to Claire. Tobias asked Claire out and they went out on a few casual dates. After just a few weeks Claire realized that she was falling for Tobias and that he was an excellent potential husband. After much deliberation and prayer, Claire decided to postpone her mission and see how things went with Tobias. They were married in April and Claire used the money she had saved for her mission for their new apartment together. By the end of the same year, Claire's younger brother was called and served in the

exact same mission in Italy.

With missions, as with all other areas in our lives, our Heavenly Father has a plan for us. Claire's preparations to serve the Lord resulted in her pursuing her own testimony and desiring to go through the temple. She wanted to serve a mission, she tried as best she could, but ultimately her choice was flexible and Claire was blessed with a husband instead. Preparing and being worthy to serve a mission is just as important as actually going because it places you in the right spiritual place to serve the Lord or your future family.

Many women wonder why men are expected to serve and women are less encouraged. In my experience with men and missions, I would venture to say it's because they have things to learn that we already know. I may be banking on a stereotype, but I believe that missions provide men training ground to learn to serve. The majority of women have been raised to be nurturers, especially LDS women. President Faust observed that being a woman "is the divine adornment of humanity. It finds expression in [our] capacity to love, [our] spirituality, delicacy, radiance, sensitivity, creativity, charm, graciousness, gentleness, dignity, and quiet strength . . . Femininity is part of [our] inner beauty."[xxii] Ever met a man-sapling under twenty-one who is self-taught in all those things? Missions are one way for men to learn graciousness, dignity, spirituality, and gentleness. Thankfully, while they're out learning to serve the Lord, they're also learning how to do their own laundry and care for themselves. Another thing men should learn while they're on missions is to be completely faithful to the cause they serve. This principle has application to their future marriages. If a man has completed a full-time mission without breaking the Law of Chastity, his fiancé will worry about his testimony and his fidelity a little bit less.

So…what about me? Should I go?

If you feel strongly that you need to go on a mission, then you should counsel with the Lord, your family and your church leaders. Do you have a burning desire to serve the Lord, then and believe that a mission is the only way to accomplish that service? Then by all means, make it a goal to go into that white field and thrust in your cute pink sickle with all your might. If you are still on the fence and not sure if a mission is for you, consider giving this decision some serious thought and prayer. Talk to other girls who have served and ask them how they made the decision to go. Also, you might want to ask women who opted out of the mission opportunity why they passed.

Deciding to serve a mission is a very personal experience. I would also suggest reading President Hinckley's 1997 General Conference talk concerning young women serving missions. I find this talk riveting because President Hinckley presented the topic during the Priesthood meeting, which may be why some women still haven't been exposed to this doctrine. The Prophet notes the sensitivity of the issue, no doubt deferring to the impressions of the Spirit for every individual woman; if a woman feels she must go and cannot shake the feeling, she should then serve a mission. The pertinent section of the talk is as follows:

Now I wish to say something to bishops and stake presidents concerning missionary service. It is a sensitive matter. There seems to be growing in the Church an idea that all young women as well as all young men should go on missions. We need some young women. They perform a remarkable work. They can get in homes where the elders cannot.

I confess that I have two granddaughters on missions. They are bright and beautiful young women. They are working hard and accomplishing much good. Speaking with their bishops and their parents, they made their own decisions to go. They did not tell me until they turned their papers in. I had nothing to do with their decision to go.

Now, having made that confession, I wish to say that the First Presidency and the Council of the Twelve are united in saying to our young sisters that they are not under obligation to go on missions. I hope I can say what I have to say in a way that will not be offensive to anyone. Young women should not feel that they have a duty comparable to that of young men. Some of them will very much wish to go. If so, they should counsel with their bishop as well as their parents. If the idea persists, the bishop will know what to do.

I say what has been said before, that missionary work is essentially a priesthood responsibility. As such, our young men must carry the major burden. This is their responsibility and their obligation.

We do not ask the young women to consider a mission as an essential part of their life's program. Over a period of many years, we have held the age level higher for them in an effort to keep the number going relatively small. Again to the sisters I say that you will be as highly respected, you will be considered as being as much in the line of duty, your efforts will be as acceptable to the Lord and to the Church whether you go on a mission or do not go on a mission.[xxiii]

And there you go. Going on mission is not essential to your "life's program", but you may go if you so chose. If you do decide to go, make sure you are going for the right reasons. I have made a list of reasons people go on missions that should never be in your top ten:

The WRONG Reasons to Serve

1. **Free food**.

   Yes, people will feed you at their homes frequently. However, they will keep feeding you until you get fat. You will remain fat unless you're on a bicycle mission. Have you ever tried to ride a bicycle in a skirt? It's a lose-lose situation. Either you're gaining weight or you're going to have to ride a bike in a skirt.

2. **To meet a husband – Lots of righteous, single men!**

   NO! Bad! There are always exceptions, but generally missions are not good places to meet future spouses. What, are you going to seduce a missionary? Dare you distract them from the Lord's work? It's hard enough for them to have purpose single to the glory of God and you're going to show up with a wandering eye?

3. **You don't know what else to do with your life**.

   Keep reading. I have plenty of great ideas about what you could be doing with your life.

4. **Everyone else in your family has served**.

   So what? This one snares a lot of women. You are not everyone else. Serving a mission is a personal decision to be made under the influence of the Spirit and with the help of priesthood authorities. You are no less of a woman if you don't serve a mission. Every member a missionary.

5. You don't want to get a job.

Talk to any RM and they'll tell you that Missions are SO much harder than a 9 to 5 job. Are you aware of the hours missionaries keep? You have to keep the same coworker around you 24/7. You have to eat with them, sleep in the same room as them, exercise with them, and should never let them out of your sight.

6. So everyone will think you're fabulous.

Prideful reason! Don't go on missions for the glory. If you do go, everyone will quit listening to you as soon as you say, "On my mission, Blah Blah Blah . . ."

7. No marriage prospects.

There is precious little time when you are young and considered marriage material by LDS men. If you take off during these crucial years, you're taking yourself off the market. While a mission may actually make you more desirable dating material, go to a Singles ward and count how many unmarried women nearing 30 are RM's. It's sad, but it's true. Often these ladies whine that all the good men are gone by the time the Sisters come home from their missions. While female RM's come home older and wiser, sometimes they're too threatening for the average LDS man (that's a challenge, in case any man happens to pick this up).

8. **Your boyfriend dumped you.**

    Get a therapist or a new boyfriend.

9. **For all the great footwear.**

    Now I know this is a very materialistic reason and a very small sacrifice to make for the opportunity to serve the Lord, but I can't help it. Missionary shoes are uglier than nurse shoes, worse than combat boots, and even more hideous than orthopedic lunch lady hush puppies. Go on a mission and commit yourself to 18 months of bad shoes.

Some of the RIGHT reasons

Serving the Lord
Preaching the Gospel
Serving others
Solidifying your testimony
Learning the scriptures
Learning about other cultures or learning a language

While these are great motivating factors for women to consider while thinking about serving missions, if you decide not to serve a mission, many of the benefits of a mission can be achieved in other ways. You can learn a language by studying at school and, even better, you can choose which language you learn. Studying abroad is a great way to learn a language and nearly every university has semester or study-abroad programs. (While you're living abroad you can actually date the hot foreign boys you meet!) Institute of Religion programs and church education offer a variety of classes on the scriptures, and many universities teach the Old and New Testaments as literature. The Church website has infinite resources for studying the words of the prophets and doctrine, as do Church bookstores. You can be self-taught in the scriptures.

Serving a mission is not the only way to solidify your testimony. Standing for truth and righteousness on the home front is as powerful a missionary means as pounding the pavement with church name badges. The lifestyle of a Mormon is different and distinct, turning everyday routine into a teaching tool. If you're living righteously, you can be a member missionary. You can be a member missionary by finding people who are looking for the gospel, being a good example through righteous living, and helping retain members by being an active participant in gospel activities.[xxiv]

Above all, unlike the choice for the men, remember that your choice to serve a mission does not define your "commitment" to the gospel. Not all good church members have served missions and not all returned missionaries remain good church members. If you feel that you have missed out by not going on a mission, remember that you will most likely have the opportunity to serve a couple's mission with your spouse when you are older and wiser.

Lastly, if the Spirit tells you to go on a mission and you've counseled with your parents, the bishop and the stake president, by all means, serve a mission. But don't say I didn't warn you about the shoes.

Resources:

- www.sistermissionary.com - All inclusive site with links for clothing and care packages. Before you go, check lists and the like.

- Women and Missionary Service by W. John Walsh. This website is non-church affiliated but has been given recognition by a variety of pro-LDS groups, such as PEARLS, The Best LDS websites and Deseret's Best

- http://www.lightplanet.com/mormons/daily/missionary/women.htm

- http://mtc.byu.edu/doc/sisters.pdf - Website from the MTC describing the Missionary Grooming Standards. Also great pictures.

- "Raising the Bar" by Ed Pinegar. Training Book by a former MTC President, informative about how to effectively teach the gospel. Note how there are only Elders on the cover.

- The October 1997 Conference Talks found on www.lds.org. This conference emphasized missionary work of all sorts.

Good Girl Goal #10: Control thy Hormones!

Before you venture out into the dating-toward-marriage world, you're going to need to commit to some personal standards of moral cleanliness. We've talked about testimonies and repentance, so we might as well identify and prepare for a major temptation facing young women of marrying age. By the time you get to your twenties, your biological (read: hormonal) clock will be a ticking time bomb. If you're serious about getting married in the temple, you need to be morally clean.

We spend our entire puberty avoiding candid discussion about sex. Well, now it's time to meet the issue head-on. (Some of you may have skipped directly to this chapter. My sisters did. For shame!) There are so many myths and misconceptions about Mormons and sexuality. Sometimes lack of discussion and accurate information can lead to sexual deviance and other problems. Sex is not talked about openly, it's associated with shame, and the way it is discussed in Young Women's is at best general, for decency's sake. Sex, therefore, is a tricky topic. We're going to talk about it anyway, and I'm going to do my best to carefully explain how I got through this one. Look out, ladies, 'cause we're going to draw some lines in the Law of Chastity sand, make a list of activities that will make you feel morally unclean, talk about harnessing your sexual prowess, examine how sex complicates relationships, identify a sexual "double standard", and list some good reasons to avoid pre-marital sex. I even threw some Shakespeare in there for good measure (and no, it's not the "to be or not to be" speech). Are you nervous? I am! Here we go!

Kate grew up in the gospel and had goodly parents who loved the Lord, as the song goes. She went to all of her young women meetings and had a lot of friends. When Kate was in her junior year of high school, she got involved with a Carter who was a member of the Church, but was inactive. Occasionally, Kate and her boyfriend would go to Church together but eventually, Carter and Kate began to be physically intimate. Kate really didn't want to have sex, but after all the fooling around, it eventually happened. Carter was ambivalent about the Law of Chastity, but Kate knew she was making the wrong choices. Every morning she woke with a sense of dread in her stomach, which she identified as the Spirit. With much effort, Kate was able to ignore the promptings of the Spirit and the guilt she was feeling. As the months went on, every time Carter and Kate became physical Kate thought to herself, "I've already messed up. Who cares if I do it again?" You can guess what happened next.

Doctor's offices are always freezing, but they're especially cold when you have to kick off your shoes and slide your tootsies into those metal stirrups. In the dead of winter, Kate had to kick off her Tommy Hilfiger boots and wait for the doctor to confirm her suspicions: she was pregnant. Kate knew hiding the pregnancy was not only difficult but also dangerous so she turned to her mother for help. Her family was horrified but supportive; Kate decided that giving the child up for adoption would be the best method.

The ordeal was traumatic and the family tried to keep Kate's pregnancy a secret, but people in the ward gossiped anyway. Bravely, Kate gave away her child and made an anxiously waiting family very happy. Nonetheless Kate was humiliated and decided to move away with Carter. They are still dating and may eventually get married, but both are inactive. Kate's mom keeps in touch with the adoptive parents who occasionally send photos of the baby who would have been her first grandchild. If Kate and Carter do get married, they will never be able to reclaim their firstborn child.

This is a bittersweet story and one every church member knows. It shows that premarital sex involves more than just the lusty, unmarried girls who mess around with it. Before Kate and Carter had sex they ought to have thought about the other people involved. Jeffrey R. Holland refers to sex as "a river of fire that must be banked and cooled by a hundred restraints if it is not to consume in chaos both the individual and the group."[xxv]

Responding to hormones is one of the easiest ways Satan can grab souls and hold them forever. Thankfully, Kate's is an extreme example and it is completely avoidable. Premarital sex is a challenge for many Saints but plenty have avoided and overcome these obstacles. It is vital to keep in mind that Kate herself is not lost; no soul ever is lost to Heavenly Father. Heavenly Father loved Kate during every stage of her progression and the Atonement is still available to her should she choose to claim that blessing. That's the miracle of the gospel. There may occasionally be pain, but there is always hope.

The Law of Chastity

The Law of Chastity means having no sexual relations except with your husband or wife. In The Proclamation to the Family, the key words regarding chastity are: "The sacred powers of procreation are to be employed only between man and woman, lawfully wedded as husband and wife."[xxvi]

Here's what you know already: Sex is only appropriate when it's with your husband within the bonds of marriage and we've been given a Law of Chastity to follow. Puzzlingly, most doctrine avoids specific identification of "chastity". There is a Law of Chastity, but it's not outlined in clear terms. There are maxims and adages (such as "always keep two feet on the floor", "keep a Book of Mormon distance between you when dancing", "the Holy Ghost goes to sleep at 10pm", etc.) but no written directions on how to live the Law of

Chastity. When I was a teen, sex was a really cloudy issue; I never felt comfortable talking to anyone about it and I never knew why.

Think about the time one of your parents attempted to give you the old "birds and bees" talk. How awkward was that? If they used "birds" and "bees" it simply didn't make sense. How do birds and bees mate, anyway? Wouldn't that result in some kind of hybrid Birdbee? If they used "penis and vagina" it was just too weird coming from your parents. It wasn't the place of church leaders to discuss sex, and while sex education at school was mildly informative, it left a real gap between the world's view on sex and the gospel's view. Sex became black and white – the world said "yes" and the gospel said "no." The first thing I read that approached the issue of the Law of Chastity was the For the Strength of Youth handbook which states:

> **Before marriage, do not do anything to arouse the powerful emotions that must be expressed only in marriage. Do not participate in passionate kissing, lie on top of another person's body, with or without clothing. Do not allow anyone to do that with you. Do not arouse those emotions in your own body.**

I'm sure we all remember the strange terminology used as an attempt to explicitly define what was not okay. They used to call it "petting and necking." I'm married and I still don't know how to "neck" or "pet." What is that? I've searched and searched but the For the Strength of Youth handbook published by the church is the most explicit definition of what's naughty and what's not. The scriptures only say "Flee fornication," and flee "anything like unto it."[xxvii] Unfortunately, the youth of the church are sometimes creative or even innovative when it comes pushing the boundaries of what is acceptable based on the guidelines they are given in Young Men's and Young Women's. The authors of the Handbook were definitely aiming to encourage youth to live the spirit of the law, and in the interest of tact, they chose not to specify the graphic details of what "anything like unto it" means. I am not so tactful and you secretly already have an idea of good personal guidelines, so they may as well be in print. Morally impurity begins here.

You are Still Breaking the Law of Chastity if You...

1. Participate in activities known in the parlance of our time as "dry docking," "Levi loving," "body surfing" or anything resembling this activity, whether laying, sitting, or standing on your head. (No loss here. You're better off for it. It sounds painful).

2. Intentionally see a member of the opposite sex naked or partially naked. No skinny dipping, changing in the same room, streaking etc. (There goes half the fun of college).

3. Engage in any kind of sexual fluid exchange or activity that could potentially result in fluid exchange. No watching either.

4. Touch or kiss anybody sexually, including yourself. I don't know how to kiss yourself, but just don't do it. That kissing and touching "anywhere that isn't covered by a bathing suit" excuse is just silly. Anywhere that isn't covered by garments is a better line of thought, and hickeys are also bad form. (That means YOU, teenagers at amusement parks!)

5. Engage in phone sex, cyber-sex, lustfully thinking about sex or any other kind of sex. Basically, no sex for you. "In other words, as we have frequently said, there should be total chastity of men and women before marriage and total fidelity in marriage."[xxviii]

Morality, fidelity, cleanliness, and purity are all ideals that are synonymous with living the Law of Chastity. I hope the above guidelines are basic enough for you not to know what to avoid. You are not expected to treat men's bodies like kryptonite – most people do some kissin' and huggin' but you must use your best judgment. Authorities leave the definition of moral purity to the individual's own conscience.[xxix] Let me put it this way: The Holy Ghost will tell you where the sex line is, and you will definitely know when you have crossed.

Raging She-Tigers!

Women are sexual animals. So are men. Sometimes we get blamed with being over-sexed and responsible for any acts of indiscretion, but that is not true. Every person has her own free agency and is responsible for falling prey to temptation; every person has the ability to flee from temptation.

That said, don't be a temptation. By temptation I mean don't be a tease. You know what I mean. Men are weak. Do you think we have dress standards because women should be ashamed of their bodies? Nope! It's because dumb old boys can't handle themselves. Being a temptation is not limited to outward appearances, it's also an attitude. You can be playful without being a tease. You can be cute without soliciting lewd behavior from guys.

Just so you know, in 2004 there were a reported 209,880 victims of rape, attempted rape, or sexual assaults, according to the 2004 National Crime Victimization Survey.[xxx] Being attractive is an extremely dangerous tool that women can choose to exploit by dangling their sexuality in men's faces. If you do not want to be a victim of unwanted attention, tone down your sex appeal and let your other unique qualities shine. Many, many girls naively overuse their sexuality to get male attention and are surprised when they develop a reputation for being easy or cheap. Having a tight leash on your own sexual power is one way to live the Law of Chastity.

You can be hot and classy at the same time. Celebrities are notoriously tasteless in their personal lives, but you sure wouldn't know it to look at some of them. The following few have made recent wardrobe selections that convey a timeless quality making them look the right kind of hot. Like them, the image that you choose to transmit through your appearance should be elegance. I'm not saying they are paradigms of refinement in their personal choices, but you've got to hand it to these gals for making Hollywood look sophisticated.

Five Hot Girls Who Convey Class

Reese Witherspoon

Jennifer Hudson

Mandy Moore

Rachel Weisz

Natalie Portman

Obedience to the Law

Ava fell in love with Isaiah when they were in college at BYU. Isaiah had returned from a mission and they were both hard at work on their degrees when they began dating. Ava had healthy self-image and was pursuing a career in advertising. Isaiah was impressed by Ava's drive, but really expected that his wife would be a stay at home mother. Despite their differences, Isaiah and Ava thought that they were in a serious relationship wherein opposites attracted. The couple was very physically attracted to each other and they eventually let temptation grab hold of them, resulting in them beginning a pre-marital sexual relationship.

When Ava and Isaiah started having sex they figured that they should "make it honest" and get married. They both knew they had made a mistake in violating God's Law so they thought that marriage would be a good next step.

The wedding came and went. Within five years Ava and Isaiah had three boisterous sons who make them both very happy. However, Isaiah and Ava have problems in their marriage because Isaiah's expectation of his wife is different than the way Ava wants to live her life. They fight a lot and are currently separated.

Ava's story is an example of how sex complicates relationships. Satan doesn't think about your long-term goals when he tempts you to be intimate with someone other than your spouse. When you chose to flout HF's Laws by having premarital sex you have a problem with obedience and sexual temptation. With those two issues rearing their ugly heads, do you think you're really in a good place to get married? Sex outside of marriage is always a huge mistake and it will be a shaky foundation for a marriage. If the person you love helps you break covenants you've made with the Lord then they are not showing love to you.

Countless women fall prey to compounding their mistakes – they think that because they've had sex they are damaged goods and should accept any man who proposes. Many girls marry the man who robbed them of their virginity simply because they feel too guilty to have any self worth. I pray for women who limit their thinking in this way. Spencer W. Kimball makes the same point,

> **My beloved youth, he is not your friend who would rob you of your virtue. She does not love you if she tempts you or yields to you. Such is your enemy. To require the yielding to passion, and gratification, yet to profess love, is to lie; for we never exploit one whom we love.**[xxxi]

Why would you feel obliged to marry a "friend who would rob you of your virtue"? To think that you must is erroneous and it shows a lack of faith in the Atonement of Jesus Christ; people do make mistakes and have to repent. If you make this "sin second-to-murder" error, do not compound your mistake by marrying quickly, out of despair, or just plain stupidly. Before you even think about getting married, you need to be able to trust your ability to keep the Law of Chastity. The Atonement is available; God still loves you and wants you to be happy.

President Ezra Taft Benson explains better than I ever could as quoted in the October 1999 Liahona:

> **There is no lasting happiness in immorality. There is no joy to be found in breaking the law of chastity. Just the opposite is true. There may be momentary pleasure. For a time it may seem like everything is wonderful. But quickly the relationship will break down. Guilt and shame set in. We become fearful that our sins will be discovered. We must sneak and hide, lie and cheat. Love begins to die. Bitterness, jealousy, anger, and even hate begin to grow. All of these are the natural results of sin and transgression.**

If you're feeling these feelings, it's time to hit your knees, and consult the proper Priesthood Authority.

One of the reasons girls give in to the temptation of sex before marriage is because they think that it will make their boyfriends feel obligated to marry them. Women and men come at this topic from polar opposite perspectives, especially in the LDS church. Even if a man wants to have sex with you and tries to talk you into it by making you promises he will usually lose respect for you if you give in to his begging. This is one of the world's ultimate double standards and for discussion on the topic, we're gonna turn to the Bard.

Yeah, Shakespeare. That's right. Love him. Even in 1604, girls were plagued by the double standard of temptation and purity, as examined in Measure for Measure. Literary circles refer to the subject as the Madonna/Whore contradiction and basically it means that women are attractive because of their purity and then expected to behave immorally. In Measure for Measure, Isabella is a symbol of purity and goodness. The local authority Angelo has condemned Isabella's brother, Claudio, to death for impregnating his girlfriend. When Isabella pleads to Angelo for Claudio's life, Angelo is attracted to her saintliness. Everything seems okay, but then Angelo tells Isabella that Claudio will be released if Isabella agrees to have a secret sexual rendezvous with Angelo.

Isabella's bind is a remarkably similar to that of girls who get caught up in premarital sex. If she goes for it with Angelo, she's committing a huge sin but she might get a "reward." In the play, and occasionally in life, sex is used as a tool in the most abhorrent way. Angelo wants her because she's pure, but intends to make her abandon the very thing that makes her so desirable: her purity. If men fall in love with you, it's because of your marvelous personality and the light of Christ you have in your life. When they expect sex, they don't think about how they will see you afterward – as someone who gave it up. You might think you're securing your a husband, but you are really using sex as an instrument to get what you want and in the process, you're lowering your status with the man you hope to keep.

Premarital sex will bring you nothing. Sex will not get you a worthy husband, it will not make anybody love you, and it will not tie anyone to you. Expect nothing from having pre-marital sex. On a related topic, no one ever needs to know anything about your adherence to the Law of Chastity. If someone has impudent cheekiness to ask, you are not required to answer. If they persist in asking you about chastity or any other law of God, an appropriate answer is always, "I don't talk about past transgression."

An excellent discussion on the Law of Chastity is Neal A. Maxwell's "The Seventh Commandment: A Shield." He introduces the topic by grounding it in Old Testament times, referring to when Jacob called the Law of Chastity a tender subject. Tender, it is. In the OT, Jacob is, "Anxious because his audience had feelings 'exceedingly tender and chaste and delicate,' Jacob did not wish to 'enlarge the wounds of those who [were] already wounded, instead of consoling and healing their wounds' (Jacob 2:7, 9)."[xxxii] How many church meetings have you been in when the topic of sex comes up and you shudder? I've sat through many. Sex is not a topic that is easily discussed publicly because it's associated with shame and hurt. Even Jacob had to be considerate because many of his congregation had tender feelings about the subject. When it comes to the Law of Chastity, many hearts are deeply affected because this law is related to creation. Jacob writes, "Many hearts died, pierced with deep wounds" (Jacob

2:35). This is as true today as it was during Old Testament times. Breaking the Law of Chastity breaks hearts and many are left with wounds that last.

Neil A. Maxwell, (whose initials spell NAM), writes, "Today we move among so many of the walking wounded, and the casualty list grows." Here are some of the effects that can occur when people give in to sexual temptation:

As if Revelation Wasn't Enough!

Reasons Not to have Premarital Sex

1. Children are born out of wedlock to unfit parents, frequently resulting in criminal behavior. "Growing up in a single-parent home roughly doubles a child's propensity to commit crime. So does having a teenage mother. Another study has shown that low maternal education is the single most powerful factor leading to criminality."[xxxiii]

2. Your sexual behavior is at risk of becoming public if you break up, potentially causing embarrassment and public humiliation.

3. Sexual activity is a slippery slope. When you engage in sinful activity you're more likely to pursue an environment and community where this behavior is accepted, thus putting you at the mercy of other temptations such as alcohol and drugs.

4. Frivolity with sexuality can lead to self-esteem issues. People who have multiple partners are more susceptible to having intimacy problems when they get into a serious relationship.

5. Having sex before marriage is like opening the floodgates - this may lead to addictive or destructive behavior such as requiring increasing amounts of stimulus for enjoyment.

6. Memories from past sexual experiences can haunt you for the rest of your life.

Nearly every family is affected by people who do not live the Law of Chastity. Every year the US government provides statistics for children born to unmarried mothers. In 2003, the overall birth rate was 45 births per 1,000 unmarried women ages 15–44.[xxxiv] Thankfully, that's up from the 1990's when there were even fewer live births.

HF loves us and He created the Law of Chastity for our protection. We are all at various points along our progression toward perfection. Be perfect in your desire to live the Law of Chastity and pray for strength to withstand Satan's assault on the family.

Resources:

- Bruce Monson, "Speaking of Kissing," New Era, June 2001, 32
- Jeffrey R. Holland, "Personal Purity," Ensign, Nov. 1998

- Brad Wilcox Growing Up: Gospel Answers about Maturation and Sex. For those of you who don't know the facts of life. It's for young people.

- Neal A. Maxwell, "The Seventh Commandment: A Shield," Ensign, Nov. 2001

- There are also a number of books on sexual intimacy in marriage, but I'm not going to tell you what they are because you don't need to know yet. If you're really interested, look up 'intimacy' on Deseret Book's website.

- The US Bureau of Justice has an office devoted entirely to Violence Against Women http://www.usdoj.gov/ovw/

- National Domestic Violence Hotline at 1-800-799-SAFE or 1-800-787-3224.

- National Sexual Violence Resource Center at 1-877-739-3895 (toll free) Familiarize yourself with RAINN: The Rape, Abuse & Incest National Network is the nation's largest anti-sexual assault organization. RAINN operates the National Sexual Assault Hotline and carries out programs to prevent sexual assault, help victims and ensure that rapists are brought to justice. www.RAINN.org

Good Girl Goal #11: Get Gorgeous, Girl!

You saw this coming, didn't you? Inner beauty is of primary importance, but making yourself as beautiful as possible on the outside is a close second. Part of having confidence is being proud of and happy with your physical appearance. I don't care where you live or what type of job you do. You're just going to have to put in some effort to be attractive. Yes, you're beautiful. Yes, you have naturally glowing skin and lovely hair. But NO, you cannot leave the house in sweats and slippers. This chapter will cover the basics of hair, skin and clothes, as well as take a skeptical look at the burgeoning culture of artificial enhancement. Bear in mind throughout that beauty is relative – you want to look like the best you, not the best imitation of a celebrity.

It's important to look like you care about yourself if you want someone else to care about you. Doing your hair and wearing make-up isn't just about making you look better, it's projecting that you care about yourself and are willing to make some effort. This is just like the exercising section – if you are trying to take care of yourself, people will believe you are worth their time. Men see women who care for themselves as potential mates. One of the things men want in their mate is someone who will project an outward appearance of cleanliness. If the woman looks put together it causes men to believe that their future homes and children will also be tidy.

It's unfortunate that society puts these restraints on women, but you're going to have to suffer through brushing your hair just long enough to get that ring on your finger. You can shave your head and burn your bra when you're married. Trust me, he'll never see that one coming.

Hair

Men love hair. It's a genetic thing. They don't even know they do it, but men associate hair with youthfulness and fertility. Even Guns n' Roses confesses, "Her hair reminds me of a warm safe place where as a child I'd hide and pray for the thunder and the rain to quietly pass me by." Sorry, Sweet Child O' Mine. You've got to grow your hair out.

When men see short hair they associate it with their mother, or worse, their grandmother. Flip through a bridal magazine or a men's mag. Find me a girl with short hair. Even if you manage to find one, I bet it's the only one. That's because men have been programmed to associate long hair with beauty.

It's really awful, isn't it? I look terrible with long hair, but when I was dating I grew out my hair so that more men would be interested in me. Men are scared of girls with short or weirdly cut hair – it makes them think that you're braver than they are. If you don't want to intimidate most men, keep your hair simple, long, and boring. It works.

You don't have to have hair down to your hips. Somewhere between your earlobes and your shoulders ought to be sufficient. Keep your hair well trimmed, too. It doesn't have to be in the exact cut of the ex-Mrs. Pitt's, but clip off the split ends. Copy someone's hair you like by bringing a picture ripped out of a magazine into a salon.

Hair color doesn't really matter, either, as long as it's not too weird. Men want to be able to introduce you to their mothers, but they won't if you have Kelly Osbourne's latest scary color. I hated this part too because I like having weird hair colors. But when I was preparing to find a husband, I had the most boring hair I could tolerate. The pony tail is a saving grace. Furthermore, dying your hair a flattering color won't kill you. Many people think that women who dye their hair are trying to be something other than the way God made them. However, highlighting and dying your hair can actually bring out your best facial features. When your boyfriend goes on about how naturally beautiful your dyed hair is, just smile and nod. Do not allow men to find a single gray hair on your head. Don't let yourself find any either, it's just too depressing.

My sister Cassandra has the most sensational highlights. She keeps them well-maintained by going to the hairdresser's once a month and they look reasonably natural. Her husband Hans has been known to ridicule women who color their hair saying that they are the height of vanity. Hans frequently points out other women to Cassandra who have disastrous highlights saying "Look! That's so artificial!" Then he praises Cassandra up and down for being so natural and beautiful. Cassandra just smiles and laughs; then makes another appointment with her hairdresser. He's none the wiser and it makes Cassandra feel great. She says hair coloring is on a need to know basis: don't ask, don't tell.

Your best bet for color is to, again, copy some hot celebrity. That way you'll avoid local pitfalls such as the zebra stripes that are finally going out of style. Another tactic is to ask your mom for her opinion. She'll tell you what your best hair looks like. Don't listen to your girlfriends, because they'll lie to you to avoid hurting your feelings and then steal your boyfriend.

Your husband will understand when you change your hair after you get married. Cassandra eventually told Hans her highlights are fake. He got over it rather quickly and praised her for being so sneaky, when it's known far and wide she can't keep a secret. I knew my future husband was the one for me when I confessed to him that I wanted my hair short and he drove me the salon and paid to chop it all off. After we got married, I dyed it pink for the summer. He's still working on that one.

Skin

Take care of your skin. For heaven's sake, wear sunblock. Men don't really care how tan you are, but if you must fake n' bake, don't allow your skin to get too orange.

By the way, I don't follow this particular advice at all. I like lying in the sun. It goes well with naps. Maybe I will dye of skin cancer and be as wrinkled as a prune, but I will die tan.

As far as skin, your face is especially important.

First issue: acne.

Learn to believe in the miracle of modern medicine. There is no reason for you to suffer with acne. Go to your general practitioner and ask for help. Acne is a problem in my family and I've run the gamut of acne medications. Two different solutions have worked for me, and they don't tear you up as much as Accutane. My best bet is Ortho-tricyclin. Yes, it is a hormone and is commonly used for birth control, but acne can be related to hormones and oral birth control really helps get everything under control. The benefits of Ortho-tricyclin are regular periods, more manageable cramps, and less acne. UCLA is still conducting surveys about mood-swings, but I didn't notice them and it cleared my skin right up. The other medication that worked is called Doxycycline. It's a low grade antibiotic and it's worked for everyone in my family, from the girls in puberty to the adults. Again, consult your doctor about it – I'm just making suggestions and I assume no legal responsibility, though I expect a thank-you card if my suggestions work for you.

Second issue: Wrinkles.

There is nothing wrong with wrinkles. Call them smile lines and get over it. I'm developing a new wrinkle. I call it my "thinkin' line" and I think it makes me look smarter and more distinguished, like gray hair for men. I don't know much about wrinkle creams, but my thirty-year-old friend uses some sort of serum from the department store brand Prescriptives. Works for her.

Make-up

You need to wear make-up.

I love it when men say, "You're so beautiful and you don't even wear make-up!" and then a week later you'll be wearing make-up and they'll say "Why don't you ever get all made-up for me?" Fools! Little they know.

Your make-up routine does not need to be complicated. All you need is:

"The Basic Three"

1) Mascara

2) Lip stick

3) Cover-up

These are your foundation. Do not leave the house without applying those three basics. Everything else is extra. If you wear mascara and lip gloss, people will think you're trying. The cover-up is for you, it will make you feel more beautiful. I just wish we could run a survey of men and ask them what beauty product they covet and wish they could wear. I guarantee they will say cover-up. Take advantage of the fact that society allows you to cover-up your blemishes! Dab it under your eyes, on your break-outs, anywhere you feel like it. Cover-up is a gift that makes you feel less ugly. You are only as beautiful as you feel, and if you've committed to The Basic Three, your self-confidence will increase. Men always talk about how they like "natural women" but what they really like is "natural make-up." Steer clear of super trendy colors (neon pink and turquoise) on your face. Make your cover-up/foundation match your neck and don't cake it on. Use lip colors that are close to your own after you bite your lips for a few seconds, or use gloss. I am jealous of girls who exclusively wear sultry red lipstick. I want a signature color! With make-up, less is always more but some is always required.

I don't work for the company, but let me tell you that Covergirl Outlast is the best lipstick ever invented. It costs like $10 at any drugstore and comes with a color applicator and a top coat gloss; MaxFactor makes one called Lipfinity. What's great about it is that it's a 12 hour lipstick. Really, they should say it's a semi-permanent tattoo because it's basically a Sharpie marker for your lips. They use it in Hollywood for kissing scenes because it works. You put on the foundation color and let that dry, and then you go over it with glossy Chapstick. Make sure you put it on carefully because you practically need paint thinner to remove it (Covergirl sells remover too) and it does start to wear off in the middle near hour 10. But those ten hours are blissful! Doesn't come off on food, napkins, men, nothing! I used to kiss one boyfriend on a lunch date and another one after dinner, without a lipstick reapplication. My husband loves life without lipstick stains. One of my favorite things to do is put Outlast on at night before I go out and when I wake up the next morning, I'm hot! Messy hair and perfect lipstick – gone is early morning no-make-up ugly girl. Just try this one, it's a ten dollar treat for yourself.

Artificial Enhancement and Dieting

Is it a do or a don't? Fix it or leave it? Eat or Diet? What about Cosmetic Surgery?

Cosmetic surgery is a source of controversy in the Mormon world. There are arguments on both sides, each with valid points.

Deborah's ward is populated with well-educated, successful women with equally successful children and husbands. She and her husband, Pete recently returned from a couple's mission and celebrated their fiftieth wedding anniversary by doing their family's temple work with their grandchildren. Pete is known around the ward as an able body and helping hand. They're really Saints and I'm rather surprised they haven't been translated. Everybody likes them and they are enjoying the fruits of a life well lived. Deborah's present to herself on her last birthday was a fantastic face lift. It was very well done and looks natural, I only knew about it because her friend happened to mention it.

Is this wrong? Maybe she's guilty of the sin of vanity? That's what people tend to think about elective surgery, but I believe that thinking is a little Puritanical. There is a fine line between self-obsession and self-improvement.

Officially, there is nothing written about the LDS Church's stand on cosmetic surgery. In fact, many worthy members have elective surgery and support their families practicing that line of medicine. However, we are warned and counseled to use caution by General Authority Jeffrey R. Holland in his remarkable and timely address "To Young Women" during the 175th Semi-annual Conference:

> In terms of preoccupation with self and a fixation on the physical, this is more than social insanity; it is spiritually destructive, and it accounts for much of the unhappiness women, including young women, face in the modern world. And if adults are preoccupied with appearance—tucking and nipping and implanting and remodeling everything that can be remodeled—those pressures and anxieties will certainly seep through to children. At some point the problem becomes what the Book of Mormon called "vain imaginations" (1Nephi 12:18) and in secular society both vanity and imagination run wild. One would truly need a great and spacious makeup kit to compete with beauty as portrayed in media all around us. Yet at the end of the day there would still be those "in the attitude of mocking and pointing their fingers" as Lehi saw (1Nephi 8:27,) because however much one tries in the world of glamour and fashion, it will never be glamorous enough.

The argument against cosmetic surgery is simple: Why change the body Heavenly Father gave you? When you get started with cosmetic surgery, it's easy to slide down that slippery slope that leads to that creepy MTV show I Want a Famous Face or one of those extreme makeover programs. Of course, Elder Holland is not going to go ahead and condemn plastic surgery. The General Authorities are here to counsel and guide us and I especially like when Holland quotes Nephi about "vain imaginations." This leaves the interpretation up to us. As in other areas of the gospel, moderation is the key when it comes to cosmetic surgery. Just like with the Word of Wisdom and diet, the gospel tells us to eat meat sparingly and other foods in moderation. I believe that this counsel applies to dieting and cosmetic surgery as well – if you're going to participate in it don't go overboard.

For argument's sake, plastic surgery is an advanced form of vanity and a desire to look like someone we are not. In Elizabethan England (the land from which sprang the Puritans and thus Pilgrims) Puritans were well known for their condemnation of anything cosmetic or aesthetic with regards to the presentation of self. Puritans condemned the Shakespearean stage primarily because the actors were in disguise, which they found to be ungodly. The term "make-up" originates on the stage, referring to how actors "make-up" their faces to be a character. J.K. Angus is one of the first to use the term in his article on Amateur Acting, "What, in theatrical parlance, is called the 'make-up'.

This has reference to the alteration made to the appearance of the face, so as to indicate youth, age, or character."[xxxv]

Make-up and surgery are both used in modern times to indicate youth. The Puritans objected to people looking anything other than they were. Take one look at the buckle hats and black garb of the Pilgrims; they were visually in stark contrast with the aesthetics of the day. The Puritans took being "in the world but not of it" to a new level.

Where does that leave LDS people who live "in the world but not of it?" Do we have to dress all in black and buckles? Thankfully, we are freed from those unnecessary standards of humility, make-up, and fashion because they are not condemned in our modern LDS society. Of course, the association between make-up and piety is archaic by today's standards, but the argument is still reasonable with regards to cosmetic surgery. The same Puritan argument of make-up used to make you something other than yourself applies to the cosmetic surgery issue. It's something to consider.

I think we can successfully be "in the world but not of it" if we use sense and conscience to make decisions about make-up and cosmetic surgery. Be realistic about these things, use wisdom, and check yourself when your flaws become "vain imaginations". Oscar Wilde reflects on imperfections in his play An Ideal Husband "When we men love women, we love them knowing their weaknesses, their follies, their imperfections, love them all the more, it may be, for that reason." Everyone has something on their body that they would like to change. Some things are changeable, others are not. Most flaws are easy to disguise, others become part of our personality signatures. Remember that part in *My Best Friend's Wedding* when Julia and Cameron are talking about the groom's tendency to suck soup through the gap in his front tooth? Julia snaps at Cameron, "A trademark move, don't touch it." Well, think of your round tummy that way.

This Girl's Life:

My sisters have teased me about being the "big nose sister" since I can remember. They effectively gave me a complex, only to be confirmed by one of the students at the Middle School where I used to teach. I was devastated. I had a big nose! I thought they were just being mean! Of course, the first thing I did was measure it. Then I took pictures of my profile and compared it to my friends. I slipped it into conversation with my boyfriend saying horribly insecure things like "Why do you keep saying you like Penelope Cruz, Sarah Jessica Parker, and Sofia Coppola? Is it because they all have dark hair and big noses? Are you trying to tell me something?"

I thought there was nothing anyone could say that would persuade me that I don't have a big nose, at least one that was too big for my face. So I had my dad's nose. Couldn't someone just be honest about it?

It wasn't until about a year ago that my vain imaginations were quelled. I was teaching school and we were working on a section about World War II. My students (most of whom were African American) were asking about how the Nazi's knew who to kill and who not to kill, especially because everyone looked white. I showed them the propaganda pictures used by the Nazis to help identify Jews. The pictures showed profiles of dark haired men and women with characteristically Jewish noses. One of my students observed, "Ms. Craven, she looks just like you! You would have been killed!"

This little comment changed my perspective. I didn't have to look in the mirror to realize that my face looked just like a female version of my father's face, he being a descendent of an Eastern European Jewish family. Of course the pictures looked like me; how dare I want to change my heritage that I wear on my face?

The way we look reflects our family. Even if you get something changed, your kids will still carry that gene and you'll have no excuse when they come asking for plastic surgery. It's important to have a realistic perspective on our bodies and remember that our bodies are temples where our spirits dwell.

That said, thinking about alterations should be a carefully and prayerfully considered operation. (pun!)

Usually people get very wrapped up in the one feature they wish they could change, to the point of their imperfection becoming an obsessive vain imagination. One look at a Hollywood Gossip magazine will show you that even the most glamorous people feel external pressure to be the thinnest girl with the biggest chest and lips. Being attractive is important, but everyone can make the body they already have into something worth noticing and something to be proud of. My mom often jokes that "Men come for the beauty, but stay for the brains." Her principles are not far off – physical beauty attracts but brains and personality make men stay. Girls with healthy self-confidence are attractive to men; learning to love yourself as you are is infinitely more attractive than bony ribs and fish lips.

Things to consider before you go under the knife or start crash dieting

1) Is it noticeable to anyone other than you?

2) Who or what is motivating your desire?

3) Is it really that big of a problem? Does it really matter in the eternal scheme?

4) Can you afford the best surgeon possible? (Don't skimp – it is your body)

5) Are you going to want other surgery if you get this done?

6) Is there any other way to fix the problem area?

7) Are you ready for a permanent commitment?

8) Can you keep your big mouth shut? Talking about cosmetic surgery is just tacky.

9) You know it hurts, don't you? It hurts a lot. P.S., people do occasionally die during cosmetic operations.

10) Two words: Joan Rivers. Can you ward off cosmetic surgery addiction?

11) Are you prepared to have your insecurity made public by fixing it?

Many, many people go through life with unattractive features and it doesn't slow them down in the least. Consider all the people who could afford plastic surgery but they don't get it. Most people don't bother and lead successful lives despite their insecurities.

Despite the fact that you can be successful without being a perfect, we are accosted on a daily basis by images of physical perfection in the form of celebrities. Tabloids track dieting celebrities and discuss who has had surgery and who hasn't; anyone who doesn't see Satan's hand in perverting the American body image is blind. Being the modern women that we are, we are faced with the challenge of actively questioning society's definition of beauty while at the same time being beautiful enough to land a husband. If you're living the standards of the gospel, you can rest assured that your spirit is shining through. But shiny spirits don't give you shiny hair. You need to take care of your physical self and wearing make-up, doing your hair, and wearing currently in-style clothes are required. Only you can decide if your self-esteem will be boosted by a little cosmetic surgery or dieting. Use some sense, don't fall prey to "vain imaginations", and for heaven's sake, make sure it's done safely and correctly.

Clothes: Yay!

The theme continues in the clothes department: TRY. Dating is the job interview of a lifetime. Consider what hangs in the balance when a man meets you for the first time: A lifelong commitment wherein you would play the role of other half. When looking for their spouse, men are as serious about assessing your candidacy as is a job interviewer looking to take on a new employee. Unfortunately, the dating game does not have a beginning and an ending time and you must be in top form from the moment you decide you want to get married. You have no idea when you're going to meet the man of your dreams so you're just going to have to be dressed appropriately 24/7. Thankfully, HF has designed that we marry right around the time our bodies are at their best. It's all downhill from here. So let's make the most of our youth, shall we? Put the dingy sweats, grubby work-out clothes, and the t-shirt you got upon your D.A.R.E. completion into deep storage. You know those girls who wear matching outfits to the gym? Quit making fun of them and pull yourself together. They're probably married and you're not. How's about a little effort?

I know this seems callous, but dating really is a job interview. Your outfits are the resume paper of life – as much as it is an affront to what you learned in Young Women's, but few men are going to invest time to see the insides of you until they think you're at the very least presentable. How much effort you put into yourself reflects how you much effort you're going to put into a relationship.

I interviewed a headhunter about this. The recruiter had been in the business over ten years, scouting out upper management executives for jobs that paid over $100,000 a year. I asked when during a typical interview he realized whether the candidate would be good for the job. He told me that he knew within the first 15 seconds whether or not they would be right. 15 seconds! What exactly can men tell about us in 15 seconds? Well, according to this recruiter, a lot more than we think.

First impressions count for a lot. Think about it. You size people up on the street in a matter of seconds and act accordingly.[xxxvi] A clean and put together appearance suggests a trustworthy and reliable person. Businesses around the globe utilize uniforms for the very purpose of regulating how employees appear to the public. You'll pull your car up in front of a restaurant and chuck the keys to a complete stranger on the curb just because he's wearing a valet uniform. The type of outfit you wear tells people how they should treat you.

Ladies, it is obvious how people feel about themselves by the way they dress. Most likely, it will be the first thing people notice about you. You can be brilliant, accomplished, righteous, beautiful inside and out, but if you don't dress the part no one is going to care.

As a liberated person, I am again required to balk at the social construct of fashion as it relates to the self. We are fashioned in the image of Heavenly Father. Job observes, "Did not he that made me in the womb make him? And did not one fashion us in the womb?"[xxxvii] Fashion originally meant to form, mould, or shape either a material or immaterial object. Job was referring to our physical (material) body – we are shaped in the image of God. However, it is up to us to fashion our immaterial selves. Since the sixteenth century the word "fashion" has also meant designing the self.[xxxviii] We design our identities by what we do, say, and wear. God gave us the canvas, we create the art. And what we create is entirely up to us. When we meet people, their first impression is always in response to our physical selves, both what HF gave us and the fashion we have layered on top of that gift. Appearances do matter and how we choose to present ourselves conveys our intentions at first glance. Thereafter we can demonstrate our identities by what we do and say.

Even the prophets advocate dressing appropriately. President Harold B. Lee taught of the important symbolic and actual effect of how we dress and groom our bodies. If you are well groomed and modestly dressed, you invite the companionship of the Spirit of our Father in Heaven and exercise a wholesome influence upon those around you. To be unkempt in your appearance exposes you to influences that are degrading.[xxxix] Being "kempt" means to be put together and aware of the images you are conveying to the public.

Do a sociological study. Walk down the street and observe what people are wearing. See if you can guess anything about their lives.

We do it all the time and it's all right. Non-verbal clues help us navigate the world. Do you want hot men navigating toward you or away from you? To keep 'em coming, you better look stunning.

Here's Where You Start

Plan A) Call your best-dressed friend. Declare a state of emergency. Have her take you shopping. She will thank you forever, you will look great and the two of you will run off into the sunset holding hands.

Plan B) You may need to buy your own new wardrobe. Buy one. Its okay, you have a job, remember?

Since I'm not there to dress you, here are some pointers. First thing you do is assess your body and choose your best feature. Buy cuts of clothing that flatter and show off that feature. The more tailored the clothing is, the more polished you will look. If it just hangs, it's probably wrong for you. Following magazine advice is very helpful, just remember you can probably get all your basics at Target and you don't need to spend tons of money at Banana Republic and Lane Bryant to copy their latest looks.

Start your new wardrobe out with a new pair of jeans. Jean cuts change all the time and are the easiest to get wrong. The best thing you can do is find a magazine spread with your body type and buy the jeans that look best on the model that is shaped like you. Even if you're heavy, fitted jeans will slim you down. Buying jeans has become nearly as challenging as the feared swimsuit buying adventure and generic jeans can ruin a perfectly good body.

There are very few items that it's okay to spend a lot of money on. With jeans, you get what you pay for. Buying whatever you've always worn at the Gap is not going to pack it anymore. The Gap cuts their jeans so that they fit everybody; you're not everybody. You need a well-tailored jean.

One of my friends has the classic Mormon wife thick buns and thighs. She hated all her clothes because she felt fat in them. We went to the high-end department store Fred Segal in Los Angeles; she flew there specifically for this purpose. Fred Segal and a few other nice department stores employ people who just sell jeans everyday. They took one look at her and prescribed her some Citizens of Humanity jeans, like they were the jean pharmacists. She wiggled into them and instantly lost ten pounds. The jeans have not come off since.

Owning a great pair of jeans is a foundation piece and can instantly update and make chic any outfit.

Shirts are easy, just buy what you like. It's hard to go wrong with shirts, but try to avoid large prints for fear of looking like drapery. Prints too close to your face are easy to get wrong and are distracting from your fabulous hair and make-up. Variety is good, don't just live in T-shirts. My mom is still trying to break me of this one. I like fitted t-shirts, ok? Get off my back. (Get the pun?) Buying three t-shirts that fit well boosts your wardrobe in that tailoring makes you look like less of a slob. Most men's t-shirts hang straight and therefore tend to look like ponchos on women. Stick to the women's section – same goes for dress shirts.

Dresses recently have been less functional for modest women, as they are nearly all strapless or sleeveless. Go retro with dresses and people will think you're artsy. Also, they might be cheaper and cuter from thrift stores or places like Buffalo Exchange. If you haven't discovered Buffalo Exchange, do. They have excellent condition used designer clothes. For church, most women are wearing skirts and tops or suits because it's so hard to find a modest dress. Classic is always a great option – black and white is reliable, easy and classy. By the by, no need to own more than three church outfits with coordinating pieces. No one notices a little recycling, so don't break the bank. Light, bright prints are great in summer for skirts, but solids seem more formal. Heels always feel more dressed up. Fashion comes and goes but classic modesty is timeless.

A Week in Fashion

Wardrobe Ingredients:

Black Fitted Skirt Suit

Black or Gray Trousers

Perfect Jeans, and your old standbys

Knee-length Skirt

Navy Track Suit and Sweats

White Button up Shirt

White T-Shirts

Seasonal Dress shirt from Limited/BR/Lane Bryant

Fitted thin T-shirt

Sparkly Shirt

Hooded Sweatshirt

Black boots

Close toe high heels

Bright colored flats

Tights

Directions for a week of successful dressing:

Sunday:

Fitted black suit from Macy's or Banana Republic (its okay to splurge on a classic suit). Crisp white shirt. Black or nude patterned tights, fishnets if you're up for it. Close toe highest heels you own, any color.

Monday:

One outfit day, same outfit for work and Family Home Evening. Wear basic trousers and seasonal shirt from the Limited or Lane Bryant. Black boots match pants, avoid brown, it's hard to match. At FHE make casual dinner or movie plans for Wednesday night with small group, including one person you've never invited before.

Tuesday:

Two outfit day, work and workout. Work outfit is again basic, tailored white shirt and knee-length black skirt. Bright shoes, if you've got 'em. Evening workout outfit is a matching tracksuit from Target; they also have t-shirts cut for women. Go easy on bright cartoon colors.

Wednesday:

One outfit, easy change for your evening outing. Black suit jacket and Monday's trousers and a fitted thin shirt from some cheap store like Rampage or Lane Bryant. For night, switch the trousers for your perfect jeans. Same bright or interesting shoes from Tuesday for night outfit.

Thursday:

Two outfits, work and workout. Sunday's outfit recycled with less fierce shoes. White t-shirt from Target and sweats that don't have elastic at the ankle.

Friday:

Two outfits, work and play. Perfect jeans with Sunday's sassy heels. Simple shirt from Gap sale. Throw on a trendy sparkly shirt for evening.

Saturday:

Back-up pair of jeans, hoodie.

Sunday:

Sparkly shirt from Friday, black skirt from Tuesday, black boots from Monday.

At this time, I need to condemn one fashion disaster: It is never acceptable to wear chunky brown Dr. Marten inspired sandals to church. Birkenstocks and casual flip flops also fall under this category. Class is back, ladies. Ditch the hiking shoes, unless you go to church on a mountain top.

Traditional fashion advice still reigns supreme in knowing what to wear. This is why classic styles are timeless and will always be in style. If you're mom isn't around to remind you, here are the keys to dressing well:

"Fashion Commandments"

Wear a slip.

Pinstripes make you look taller and thinner.

Cartoons are only for children, not for you.

Expensive does not mean better.

Heels dress up any outfit.

No nylons or socks with open-toe shoes.

Hurty shoes are worth it, beauty is painful.

Coats go out of fashion every two years. Buy one new one.

Matching underwear makes you feel special, even though no one sees it.

Don't over accessorize.

Ross, Marshall's and Target have great cheap clothes.

Simple is always more attractive.

No white shoes after Labor Day.

Get a signature scent from a Department store.

If you don't feel fabulous, change your outfit.

Resources:

- If you're remotely interested in plastic surgery, the most amusing celebrity website is www.awfulplasticsugery.com

- Pick up any tabloid. It's a plastic surgery circus out there.

- Naomi Wolf *The Beauty Myth: How Images of Beauty are Used Against Women*. In the U.S. the average woman is 5'4" and weighs 140lbs. This National Bestseller rejects the unattainable beauty standard projected by American culture.

- Linda Mason *Makeup: The Art of Beauty*. Fun makeover textbook.

- Trinny Woodall and Susannah Constantine *What You Wear Can Change Your Life*. Style manual for women of all shapes and sizes, not as judgmental as the show What Not to Wear.

- www.buffaloexchange.com. Trendy recycled clothing store, a step up from D.I.

- Jeffrey R. Holland "To Young Women" October 2005 Conference

- Douglas Bassett, "Faces of Worldly Pride in the Book of Mormon," Ensign, Oct. 2000

Good Girl Goal #12: Be the "It Girl"

If you've been busy getting a distinguished education, an absorbing job, having scores of wonderful friends, an enviable collection of footwear, spit polishing your lustrous testimony, and inventing some intriguing hobbies, you may forget to pick up a husband. Not to worry. I'll share some techniques. We're going to learn how to be an **It Girl** by learning the how the right attitude and confidence makes you desirable. Also, we're going to air a free-style dating technique that protects hearts and uses time efficiently.

On Clarissa's twenty-fifth birthday, her mother Janice called to wish her a happy day. Clarissa was excited to tell her mom all about the latest concert she went to and her recent pay raise at work, but Janice edged toward a hazardous topic. Janice, being a typical LDS mother, could not resist the urge to ask Clarissa about her marriage prospects. Expecting Clarissa to mention a variety of men she found kind of interesting but no real serious relationships, Janice was surprised by Clarissa's response to the indiscreet questioning. Clarissa said, "Mom, I am living by three rules. I am active in church, my life is the best I can make it, and I am faithfully patient that Heavenly Father will show me my husband in his own due time. When that happens, you'll be the first to know. Quit worrying and have a little faith."

"Okay," Janice replied, "Go put your birthday Betsy Johnson wedges to work!"

If you've been following *Good Girl Goals*, you should have all your "being dateable" groundwork accomplished or in the process of becoming so. If your life is full, you are interesting. If your testimony is in order, you glow. You have an education, you have a job, you're doing something to save the world, you have a bunch of hobbies, you exercise, and you have a wardrobe that makes you feel hot and a little bit of foundation to cover the flaws. You, my friend, are ready for action. In order to share your sparkling personality and fantastic life you need a game plan. You need some dating goals and strategy. The gospel is all about progress toward a specific goal, so why not apply that line of thinking to dating?

Attracting men is all about attitude and confidence. Nearly any woman could land any man, provided she has laid her foundation and knows how to work it. We've talked all about the marvelous person you need to be, but now we need to handle the nitty-gritty of the opposite sex. Thus far, we've concentrated very little on them and focused on making ourselves everything that we can possibly be, short of joining the army. You know the girls who seem to have every man in the ward checking them out and wanting to get with them? Well, you're going to be one. It can be taught, and it's really not that hard. It's all about attitude and confidence.

A Word on the Opposite Sex

They're kind of dumb. Nay, not dumb, just misguided when it comes to women. Beyond the physical, men don't know which girl to want. Even if a girl's laid the foundation by making herself fabulous, men cannot be expected just to come running. Guys are not that bright and so women need to tell men what to do. Secretly, I think every war ever won has been because the men in charge had some bright wife telling them what to do. When it comes to dating, women are in charge of guiding men toward the best target. P.S., the best target is YOU.

Honestly! Most men are space cadets who follow where the crowd is going, even if it's headed dangerously close to the halfwit, though physically well-endowed, Barbie. They have been programmed to think a certain way and need a bit of a jolt now and then. You are that jolt. They have no idea how incredible you are until you waltz on over there and make them notice.

How does a girl get a man to notice her?

I interviewed a number of men and not a single one said "She looks like a model." Yes, I assume that helps a lot of girls, but confidence and attitude go a lot further in the long run. Here were some of the responses to the age old question:

What would make you notice a woman?

First answer: Her confidence.

Second most popular: Her attitude.

Third: She seemed hard to get.

Attitude

Men are still boys at heart. They will fall for any girl they think is fun. Have you seen the movie *King Kong*? What woman was able to tame the beast? The woman who smiled while doing back flips and cartwheels! King Kong stormed around like a crazy fool until he was taught what to like. Now, I am not suggesting that you go to clown school in order to get men (or apes) but we can learn something from Naomi Watts' attitude and confidence. You too can tame men if you make a concentrated effort to guide them towards you.

I know this girl Emilia who is just not that cute. She doesn't have a real job, her body is not proportionate, has bland hair, and average features at best. Men love Emilia. Her man-catching efficiency drove the rest of us crazy, that is, until I realized her secret. Emilia has a great and covetable attitude. She has big "hindquarters", but she has so much energy and lavishes praise on everybody. She's the very definition of bubbly. Women want to crack her upside the head, but men want to marry her. While at first

I couldn't stand her, I came to love her quirky and fun personality because anywhere she goes, she is the life of the party. Rather than glare at her, I studied her. She says whatever is on her mind, laughs a lot, and never says anything bad about herself or anybody else. For these reasons, Emilia is a great success. She spreads fun, energy, and enthusiasm. Emilia goes to all the ward activities, has tons of friends, and seems very happy. I have no idea if she is as happy as she seems, but the image of herself that Emilia conveys to others is very effective. Emilia's alluring attitude and confidence eclipses all her flaws and makes her very attractive.

1. **The Attitude of Attraction: Grab Some Spotlight.**

Taking social risks including everything from speaking up in Sunday School to volunteering to be a magician's assistant makes you a more interesting person and gives men opportunities to get to know your stunning personality.

2. **Say Something Nice.**

Saying funny or nice things is always an easy conversation starter. Church hymns encourage this all the time (did your mother go around shouting "let us oft speak kind words to each other" or was that just mine?) and using the advice of the hymns in your daily life reflects the sweetness of your personality. Compliments are always welcome conversation and everybody has something worth complimenting. People want to be noticed and appreciated – fill this social need and reap the benefits. Saying nice things does not mean saying boring things. You can be interesting, funny and nice at the same time. Also, men like it when you compliment them on their watches. It's the man equivalent to fabulous shoes.

3. Smiling + Laughing = Sense of Humor?

Laughing and smiling are both more important than being funny. Men want a good audience so that they can shine; why not capitalize on that knowledge? Laughing and smiling a lot are easily mistaken for having a good sense of humor, even if you're just secretly laughing at how lame and predictable men are.

4. Don't take it too seriously.

Dating is supposed to be fun. Make sure to remember how ludicrous the whole mating game really is and you'll be sure to enjoy what might be the silliest time of your life. Think about it. The whole concept of dating has to be the greatest joke HF has played on us since the duckbilled platypus. Remember the last Singles social gathering you attended? Chances are the activity was just an absurd excuse to get people of similar age and opposite sex in the same room together and even then successful matchmaking was as difficult as nailing jelly to a tree. Singles Wards are a hilarious social experiment. Someday when you're old and married, you and your husband will laugh all about the things you said, people you met, and activities they dreamed up. A talent show full of grown people? Ice blocking? Sober Karaoke? I mean come on! Have a good attitude, take it as it comes and enjoy it while it lasts.

Confidence

Men dig it. Confidence is an easy thing to fake. Even if you don't feel confident at all, you can pretend you're full of confidence and it won't make a lickin' difference. Not that you don't have every reason in the world to be happy and confident. I mean, you're an independent woman with a million hobbies that keep you happy, why shouldn't you be confident?

What is confidence? Confidence is believing in yourself. Confidence is having self worth and knowing it. Elder Glen L. Pace of the Seventy quoted President Hinckley speaking of confidence:

> **I believe in myself. I do not mean to say this with egotism. But I believe in my capacity and in your capacity to do good, to make some contribution to the society of which we are a part, [and] to grow and develop. … I believe in the principle that I can make a difference in this world, be it ever so small.**[xl]

The world is at your fingertips so be happy about it and let it show. If there is anything in your life that causes you to grumble and air your complaints to others, change it. You are in control of your life. Further, you are only as confident as you choose to be. Being sure of yourself is dependent on whether or not you have purpose in life. Having purpose means that you have people who count on you, you have goals, you have a charitable heart, and, moreover, you have a desire to do the will of the Lord. Did you forget that the will of the Lord is that we be happy? Women are that they might have joy, and joy goes hand in hand with confidence.

Invite people to get to know you by speaking to them. Have no fear about initiating conversation. Everyone needs a friend and everyone is interesting in some way. Learn to study and be interested in the human condition. You have nothing to lose and a world to gain.

My dad has a lot of confidence. He talks to anyone he feels like and makes a lot of friends that way because he asks people about themselves. He's sure of his approach and isn't offended when people don't want to talk to him. He keeps trying, frequently to the point of being annoying.

Missionaries have tons of confidence. They are sure that the gospel is necessary for everyone and this gives them the confidence they need to talk to people. Confidence is a state of certainty or surety, and you can be sure that your goal of being married in the temple is in line with the will of HF. If you try to achieve this goal by talking to men and being your best self in front of them, HF will help things proceed as they should.

PLAYING Hard to Get vs. BEING Hard to Get

Making the decision that you are ready to get married is another step towards the altar. It's easy to talk about marriage with boyfriends who come and go, but when you decide that you're done with casual dating, it's time to move on to the serious stuff. Hopefully you have fulfilled most of your personal goals by this time and you're ready to think about joining forces with a competent and worthy husband who has done the same.

This Girl's Life:

When I made the decision to get married, I also decided that I was done pursuing friendships with men and done having exclusive boyfriends. I had a tendency to get into exclusive relationships which were like being engaged without the proposal, ring, or promise of real marriage. Some girls have boyfriends who eventually propose, but most girls I know who have boyfriends find themselves in relationships where men have no pressure to take the next step. This is a precarious position for a girl: She can either wait around for some catalyst to encourage her man to propose or she can use ultimatums such as "If you don't propose by this day, I'm breaking up with you." In exclusive relationships, the "chase part" of dating that men love so much is simply gone.

When I finally discovered that having a single boyfriend was a state of stagnation, I changed that tendency and dated more than one guy at a time. I found that I was weeding through them more quickly and not wasting time on relationships that were not going anywhere. My mantra was, "You're not my boyfriend." Guys hated this but it sent the message that I was only going to be serious about someone who was serious about marrying me.

The "you're not my boyfriend" attitude is not hostile – it's a gesture of freedom. Instead of playing hard to get, be hard to get! Avoiding boyfriend relationships is just one method of dating toward a purpose. There is no reason to be in a committed relationship unless you have a ring on your finger. He is allowed to date other women and you are allowed to see other men. Remaining uncommitted keeps the chase going for the guy – if you're his girlfriend there's little encouraging him to propose.

Guys who want you to be their exclusive girlfriend but aren't ready to get down on their knees and beg for your hand in marriage are *Red Herrings*. Avoid them! They will suck your best years away! They want all the benefits of a fiancé, the security and love but without the commitment. Be unwilling to be his girlfriend and tell him you're not interested in keeping one man company; you want a spouse. Girlfriends are expected to be available anytime he calls, make their boyfriend their first priority, and might even be expected to help with his stupid errands and chores. If he wants someone to do those things, he can pony up the diamond. Until then, live free! You'll run less risk of severe heartache if you quit having exclusive boyfriends, and you'll save yourself a lot of time while still remaining slightly out of reach until he just can't stand it anymore and has to propose.

The summer before Grace was married she was dating two guys in order to figure out who was the best fit. Sometimes Grace would have to hurry home from one date with Liam to find her next date, Orlando, waiting to pick her up and take her somewhere else. Grace kept no secrets; she was not trying to be sneaky. She would tell Liam that she had plans that evening, but that they could meet up the following day. If Liam wouldn't leave her apartment, then he got to greet Orlando at the door. It was always very uncomfortable, but also kind of funny. Once, Grace's dad called while she was with Orlando and asked Grace why she was with Orlando if she was supposed to be seeing Liam the next day. Grace's dad didn't understand but Grace was just hedging her bets. Her dad asked her how she planned to handle the two guys. She thought about it for a moment, looked over at Orlando and replied to her dad, "Well...may the best man win!"

Dating around is difficult and I recommend being a little more discreet than Grace without being downright sneaky. If you explain to your admirers that you're not committing to one man because it increases everybody's chances of heartbreak, they are a lot more understanding and might admit that they are doing the same thing. It bugs me that women are socially discouraged from proposing or initiating discussions about marriage. I think Grace's tactics are genius! Grace discovered that when she had a serious boyfriend she became obsessed with whether or not they were going to get married. Women have no control over when men decide to propose marriage so why limit yourself to waiting for one guy to propose?

Being honest and having integrity about your dating methods is in everybody's best interest. When it's time to get serious with one of your guys, the ball is invariably in their court.

Orlando became quickly annoyed with Grace's penchant for multiple dates. Within three months he brought up the subject of marriage and Grace told Orlando that she'd heard that line from boyfriends since she'd graduated from high school. Men lord engagement over girls and use it to get what they want: a concerned, loving pseudo-fiancé who will wait years for him to propose. Grace said she'd even had a boyfriend who bought a ring and never gave it to her! Imagine the trauma! Grace told Orlando she just wasn't going to be serious until somebody got down on his knees and gave her a diamond.

Cleverly, Orlando shot back with, "I'll give you a diamond ring as soon as you quit dating around." Grace agreed saying, "Fine. You have one month, then I'm outta here." Wham! Diamond on her finger. Grace challenged Orlando, he challenged her right back, and they both lived happily ever after.

It's one thing to think of yourself as hard to get, it's another thing to actually be hard to get. "Playing hard-to-get" is a misnomer, "being hard-to-get" is a lifestyle. You're looking for your lifetime mate, no playing around about it. Having a serious boyfriend is playing at being engaged. Quit playing and start sifting through all the options. Be creative and allow HF to surprise you with your eternal mate. Go out with everyone! The more guys you date, the better educated you will be when you finally make a selection. Elder LeGrand Curtis said, "It seems to me that this dating, courtship, and marriage process is like baking bread: it needs careful measuring, sifting, and mixing. Then it needs time to rise. Then, finally, it's ready for the oven." [xli] Now if we could only get the men baking us bread on dates that would be something! I encourage you to find a method of dating that works for you so that you can take a load off about finding a husband. And don't be mad at HF for not delivering your husband right away. You're just gonna have to sift through more wannabes until your husband shows up. Do the best you can with what you've got and pray for guidance to find a winner.

Resources:

- Dale Carnegie How to Win Friends and Influence People. This classic text will open your eyes to social interaction and teach you how to be an engaging contributor. Don't let the manipulative title fool you, Carnegie conveys sincerity and a genuine interest in positive human relationships.

- Sterling W. Sill of the First Quorum of the Seventy, "The Miracle of Personality," New Era, Mar. 1978, 5. It's an oldie, but a goodie – a successful business man talks about Ghandi, attitude, and how greatness comes to those who want to succeed.

- Glenn L. Pace of the Seventy, "Confidence and Self-Worth," Ensign, Jan. 2005, 32

- Steve Nakamoto Men are Like Fish: What Every Woman Needs to Know About Catching a Man. Amusing quote-ridden handbook from a man's perspective, including 101 things a woman can do that will send a man running for cover.

- Dr. Barbara DeAngelis The Real Rules: How to Find the Right Man for the Real You. DeAngelis has created an excellent modern woman's reaction to Ellen Fein and Sherry Schneider's The Rules (which made my stomach turn because it advocates playing games and being manipulative to find a man.)

- Marie K. Hafen, "Celebrating Womanhood," Ensign, June 1992, 50. Sister Hafen lists five goals for women: becoming somebody who can support herself, being careful while choosing your husband, becoming capable of being a good mother, living a rich life, and being spiritual. She's smart, I like her!

Good Girl Goal #13: Showing up on the Radar

College Senior Peggy first noticed Alex when he came in late to her Botany lecture. Alex was gorgeous but also happened to be tardy on a regular basis. Even though the class also had 103 other students, Peggy made sure the seat next to her was available so that Alex could conveniently sit down next to her when he came in late. The weeks wore on and Alex would always schlep to the back of the classroom to sit by himself. Without being too much of a stalker, Peggy noticed that Alex went to his locker after class before he hit the gym to tone his bronzed triceps. After casing Alex's classroom behavior for a few days, Peggy developed a plan.

Peggy found the custodian of the lockers and asked how she could get one for her own gym clothes. Using shrewd preparation, 5'4" Peggy managed to sweet talk the manager into giving her the highest locker in the bunch, ideally located directly above Alex's locker. Next, little Peggy bided her time.

Finally, it was class day again. Again, Alex sat in the back. Peggy was ready. When the lecturer finally finished, Peggy waltzed over to her newly acquired locker and asked the hot "stranger" if he could help poor little

her put her bag in her locker. Alex grinned at the cutie soliciting his

assistance and helped Peggy with her bag. "I wonder how I'll ever get it out

again," Peggy mused like a clever damsel in distress. Alex told her he'd be

back in an hour if she happened to be around. Guess what. Peggy was

waiting. They got married.

Peggy was smart. Even though she was cute and had all the personality that Alex (or any guy, for that matter) could have wished for in a wife, she was not directly in his line of vision. Sometimes men don't know who's right for them until they're told. That's why we're here. To tell them.

Even when men are actively looking for a wife, they only bother looking straight ahead of themselves. Why do you think girls wear glitter? Because, like small children, men notice bright attention grabbers. You will not land a husband if you don't put yourself into his line of vision. Your days of being a wall flower are over. That only worked for Molly Ringwald in *Pretty in Pink*, and she mostly attracted geeks with headgear.

Being in the right place at the right time is an efficient way to maximize your pool of men to marry. "The right place" to find a husband is not just in your hometown. We've talked about living the most auspicious area in the Moving chapter, and about expanding your horizons in the hobbies section.

This chapter will teach you how to land yourself on a man's radar, discuss the merits and drawbacks of online dating, provide some online rules, and make some suggestions about dating geography. Putting yourself in the right place is crucial for successfully bagging a husband.

Mission Control, We Have Contact.

Having confidence, a radiant attitude and being in the "line of fire" are all effective ways to get noticed by the right kind of man. You can certainly initiate contact. We're not exactly women who sit around and wait.

This Girl's Life:

When I first spotted the man who would end up being my husband he was sitting in Sunday School in the Singles Ward. I had been an active member in that ward for about a year and could at least recognize nearly all the regulars in the ward. I had been through my share of boyfriends and made the decision that I was going to get married within the next year 'cause I was tired of waiting. I could spot a good-looking newcomer in a moment, and there was one sitting right there in my class. My future husband had the location rules down: He was at church during the second hour, which meant that he was not just a one-meeting loser, and he was sitting alone next to empty seats on the end of a row. I sat right down next to him and watched him tinker away on his Palm Pilot during the class. Finally, I leaned over

and asked him if he was playing Tetris or something, and he laughed. He was

actually reading the scriptures. Then we got married and lived happily ever

after.

"Strategery". Thank you, George Bush Jr., for that glorious invent-a-word. Strategically positioning yourself will give you the highest chance of success. Using strategic philosophy works in all areas of life. Choosing a husband is like buying a house: you're making a lifetime commitment. Realtors will tell you, "location, location, location." Church and church activities are always the right place to be, but school and work are also fine places to meet men. Getting what you want is all about finding the angle and then setting yourself up as the best option. If you've followed the steps, you've already made yourself the best option, now situate yourself accordingly. Get in there and get your hands dirty. It's not half as hard as you think. There are many opportunities to use strategic placement to meet men and the easiest is a strategy based on principles used in the elementary school cafeteria. You've got your tray full of delicious food. Time to choose a seat.

The easiest way to get a man to take notice of you is by sitting right next to him. You don't even have to say anything at all. He's sitting for a snack on a work break. Sit down in his line of sight. If he's sitting at church, sit on down next to him close enough to have to share a hymnal but without sitting on his lap. He's guaranteed to say something to you, even if it's just "get off my scriptures."

Positioning yourself close to him makes you available in the best way possible. Men are wimps and need an "in" to strike up a conversation. If you're forever huddled with your girl posse you become an extremely difficult person to approach. It's easier to begin a conversation with someone who you have already exchanged wordless communication (eye contact, smile) as this will assure him his pathetic attempt at talking to you won't be shot down.

Another way to improve your strategic positioning is to sit by yourself and people watch. This is another non-threatening position because it allows people to approach you. People-watching is a socially acceptable sport and if you sit and smile at men as they walk by you have tremendous opportunities to send welcoming non-verbal communication. If a man decides to say something to you, it will be relatively low-risk for him because it's an easy conversation starter:

Him: What are you doing?

You: People watching, want to join me?

No one else will hear his pathetic excuse to talk to you because you're sitting by yourself, and he doesn't have to ground himself next to you if the conversation crashes and burns.

Also, one of the most fun things to do in a Single's Ward is sit and watch people. I think that's why they have couches set up in the foyers. I made so many friends sitting on that couch in the main foyers at church – they just seem to invite friendly conversation. Furthermore, I discovered that just about everyone is a little uncomfortable between classes at church and even at activities during the week. If I sat by myself, it provided a safe opportunity for people to speak to me because I didn't appear to already have a social circle. Being a lone agent is the best way to meet a variety of people. You don't have to say much, you don't have to look like you're headed somewhere important; you just get to sit and wait for somebody to come show you how terrific they are.

Making eye contact is another easy non-verbal act that opens up doors of availability. You can be all the way across the room, make eye contact for three seconds, and have a boyfriend by the end of the night. Generally this move is reserved for clubs, but it's a powerful female tool. Remember that part of Arthur Golden's *Memoirs of a Geisha* when the heroine glances at a man and makes him drop what he was carrying? This can be you. Men just don't expect such forward behavior, but it's so easy to look for three seconds at a man and lure him into coming over to talk to you. You can wink, stick out your tongue, smile seductively, or cross your eyes, but the three second look is about as effective as shouting across the room "You're hot! Come over here!" You didn't have to say anything at all. These men aren't in high school anymore – there aren't any social punishments for lookin'. I assign you to read *Memoirs of a Geisha* to improve your "come hither" technique.

When you were in high school, church leaders encouraged group dating. This is no longer necessary when you get into your twenties – you're eventually going to have to pair off with one guy to get to know him better. Double dating is fine during the initial stages of getting to know each other, but people in Singles Wards frequently abuse the group dating thing to avoid having to commit to couplehood. Group dating is fine for initial safety, but you're going to have to make the leap to dating on your own. You're a big girl now. You don't need all of your girl-friends around to help you with your dating. The *Good Girl* who dates men one-on-one ends up being the one throwing the bouquet.

LDSvixen2007: R U my husband? LOL.

Some girls attempt to bypass the difficulty of the initial contact with the opposite sex by screen-name soliciting. Online dating, baby. Ldssingles.org,ldsplanet.com, lds-please-marry-me.com, sweetcyberspirits.com – there are so many online dating sites out there, what's an eligible woman to do?

Online dating has its merits and its drawbacks. There are as many success stories as there are horror stories. There are couples who meet online and find themselves in successful marriages, and there are people who invest time and emotion into pranksters. Online dating is a gamble and one that is potentially as addictive as online gambling sites.

My basic theory of dating is that the Lord will provide after you do everything you can. If you follow the guidelines mentioned in this book, you should have your hands full and won't need to bother with online dating. Yet, more often than not, girls seek refuge in cyberspace. The reason? Because it is the lazy way to meet men. I am not saying that you're a bad person for dating online. I am just saying that what you sow you will eventually reap. I know this is a bold statement but consider: The motivations that might propel you (and your cyber-guy) toward online dating could be signs of problems in your life, such as a lack of confidence (see "Be the It Girl"), or maybe it's time to move to a fresh pond-o-men.

So you have all the confidence in the world, say you? Mr. Righteous hasn't come along and you think cyberspace will yield a greater selection of men? Keep in mind that the traditional methods of meeting people are tried and tested as well as reliable. Meeting people through church, family, friends, work, or other social activities provide face-to-face contact with enough men to make a reasonably sized dating pool. Further, the Lord has a plan for you: His pool of eligible men is deep and He could wring one out for you if the time was right. If you run out of local options, the Internet is a really tempting place to meet men but should be considered carefully.

Here are some questions you need to ask yourself before you put any real information about yourself on the Internet:

10 Questions about Cyber Love

1. Why are these people on the Internet looking for love?

Ask one hundred online daters why they date online and you'll get a hundred different answers ranging from, "I don't have time to date" to "with a digital camera and PhotoShop, I can lose ten pounds and grow an entire head of hair." Regardless of the reason they give you, deep down inside, they all chose online dating for one primary reason: anonymity. When you are online, you can be anyone, from anywhere, and say whatever you want with very little accountability. This is not to say that everyone who dates online is pretending to be someone they aren't, but I guarantee that some part of them wants to remain anonymous: whether it be their height, weight, the fact that they still live at home, don't want their girlfriend to know they're playing the field, they're not quite over their checkered past, they lack a testimony, or that they are a 'Dungeons & Dragons' Grand Wizard and still play with Legos. C'mon, you know you've made fun of online dating at least once in your life because you know that it is basically The Ringling Brothers meets the Wild, Wild West. Anything can happen. Just ask yourself this question: Do you really want to join their ranks? Is it already time to raise the white flag?

2. Couldn't they find love the traditional way? Why not?

Maybe they live in population-zero towns. Maybe you do too. Maybe there aren't any eligible men where you live. (But there are men everywhere). Have a little faith in yourself and a little faith that HF will drop a good man in your lap if you're doing everything right. Or, just move somewhere and fish in a new pond. Who knows what kind of people are cruising the Internet? Maybe they have a great profile and are chat-Jedi, but what if they secretly don't wear pants? How do you know?

3. **Where are their real-life friends and why do they make time for cyber-friends?**

Be honest. If your friends found out you were dating a stranger online, don't you think they'd give you a hard time about it? Would you hide it from them? That's rather dishonest. Conceivably, these people are doing the same thing. Does anyone admit to online dating? It can be very secretive. Being secretive on the computer can be addictive and tantalizing because nobody's watching so you don't feel accountable. Would you trust your relationship with a man who dated women online? How do you know he doesn't have three or ten secret online relationships going on at the same time? Maybe he even has a real-life girlfriend? You don't know the same people, so how could you know?

4. **Didn't your mom ever tell you not to talk to strangers?**

NO! Everybody is NOT doing it! There are still people out here who find Internet dating to be the lowest form of dating. Would you place a personal ad in a newspaper? Would you answer one? The answer is no, you would not.

Why? Because it's weird and it's dangerous! Just because it's free does not mean it's a good idea. If you bring some chap you met online home for Thanksgiving dinner, I hope you know that everybody is going to introduce him as the guy you met online. You will be branded whether you like it or not. Furthermore, if you break up the guy will fade off into oblivion. So much so that you could end up dating his brother (or his dad!) and not even know it. You don't know them, and you don't know anyone they know because otherwise you would have met already.

5. **Is there anyway you'd be embarrassed if the person you're chatting with turns out to be your dad, or your bishop?**

Face it; you could be talking to anybody! You could be talking to your married neighbor or your fifth grade teacher and not even know it! People can save the conversations you have online by a simple click of the mouse. Do you want all your innuendo saved on someone's hard drive? Do you want the foundation of your relationship to exist in a written format? If you type something to somebody you create a lasting record that can be forwarded to embarrassing sources. Don't let your flirtations come back to haunt you.

6. **Does witty small talk warrant placing yourself in danger of meeting a veritable stranger?**

Okay, fine. You've ignored me and wrangled yourself up a charming, homespun Internet cowboy. You've been talking for months; you write and chat every day. Doesn't mean he's not a member of a gang of pirates waiting to sweep you off your feet and into the back of a creepy white windowless kidnapper van, rape and pillage you and your bank accounts, extort money from everybody you know, and ruin your favorite pair of strappy heels. Until you know his family, three friends, and maybe even one ex-girlfriend, you don't know who this guy is. Be safe, or be sorry.

7. Have you ever Googled yourself?

Googling means typing your first and last name into www.google.com. Any information available about you on the Internet will come up for all to see. Nobody ever told me that much of what's online is permanent. I submitted a glowing review of a concert I saw when I was fourteen, in which I described the event as "life changing and angelic." For the last ten years when you Googled my name that little review came up. It has proven very embarrassing. Be careful what you type online. Be careful when you use your real name, address, or any other personal details.

8. Have you ever heard a band's music, fell in love with the lead singer, and then seen his picture and wanted to vomit?

You can be in love with some one from afar, but you just can't imitate a real meeting. The way someone moves, smells, acts and generally the person that they are is only evident when you meet them. Would you hire someone without conducting an interview? Why then would you call them your boyfriend if you've never smelled their cologne?

9. Are you really, really that desperate?

Well, are you? I'm sorry to put it all out there in black and white, but I just can't help encouraging you to ask yourself the questions that are potentially uncomfortable for the Internet dater.

Almost everybody has gone on at least one of these sites just to see what they're all about. You may have even invented a fake online profile to get better access to search for your friends. You may have found your friend and been tempted to tease them about their online picture (okay, I did this. Sorry, Becca!). This is surely taking it a step too far, but there is a fair measure of appropriate curiosity associated with what seems like an endless supply of "profiles" just waiting to be perused. This "cyber super-meat market" makes the number of prospects at the BYU Cougar Eat at lunchtime look like deli meat selection at 7-11.

Think of all the men out there! The world is at your finger-tips, and you can just click until one looks like your future mate. And then . . . what happens? He chats a good game, you exchange photos, you talk on the phone, and you even plan a meeting in a well-lit safe Mormon equivalent of a coffee shop (side note, what is the Mormon equivalent of a coffee shop? Brits have their pubs, heathens have their coffee shops, and what do LDS folks have? Nothing! Ice cream stands to make us fat! It's a conspiracy, I tell you. Is the Word of Wisdom intentionally associated with casual meeting places? At least we don't walk around with beer and coffee breath. After I write this, I'll open up a warm chocolate shop. Not hot chocolate, which would be a hot drink. Tepid chocolate. $3.95 a cup.) Where were we? Oh yes, you're meeting with your future stalker, no, suitor.

Imagine the possibilities of meeting up with some random from the Internet. Yes, they are still randoms, even if you met them on an LDS website. When you finally meet them, it will be weird.

Akemi fell deeply in love with her online chat buddy, Jack. After speaking on the phone for hours at a time, Jack finally decided to make the trip out to Houston to see Akemi. When Jack arrived, it took them a little while to get used to each other. Even though they had been talking daily, Akemi was a little shocked by in-person Jack.

First of all, Jack was a good four inches shorter than his online profile reported. Secondly, Jack's voice was much higher pitched than how he sounded on the phone, and he was not half as clever. Jack's idea of fashion was to wear the same acid washed jeans he wore in high school during the eighties and he didn't laugh exactly. He tittered. Furthermore, Jack had a lazy eye and he smelled of sauerkraut.

Jack wasn't dishonest with Akemi on the phone, and in cyber-space he just highlighted the good and brushed aside the bad. He didn't outright lie, he just stretched the truth (4 inches) to make himself seem desirable to a knockout such as Akemi.

Akemi was in a bind. She had feelings for Jack, but was not attracted to him physically. Moreover, Akemi discovered that Jack had everything from the Golden Formula for dating before she determined whether or not Jack was someone she would want to date. Now, some people would think that this is just great: Finally, someone like Jack has a chance with a girl who would otherwise be totally out of his league. Even though Akemi had feelings for Jack, she worried that her friends and family would fall down laughing if she brought this guy home – they wouldn't be able to experience anything but Jack's exterior and pungent aroma.

In a desperate attempt to reconcile Jack's exterior with his interior, Akemi gave Jack a man-makeover. She became his style consultant and dietitian. It took months before Akemi was ready to introduce Jack to her family and friends.

Sunday night dinner was the setting for the big introduction. Akemi had spoken so much about her online dream guy that the family was expecting a Steve Young look-alike. Upon his introduction to Akemi's father,

Jack smashed the man's hand between his palms and said, "Good to meet

you. Did Akemi dress you up too?"

You may succeed in bringing home a potential spouse you've met on the Internet, but there is no guarantee that this guy's going to know how to behave in public, or in any arena other than in front of a computer screen.

Even if things look great online and sound great on the phone, nothing can make up for face-to-face interaction. You have no idea how you're going to react to somebody, even if you're practically in love with them from a distance. Online dating is usually a charade of contrived banter that usually does not hold up come meetin' time. You've set a high standard that no one can maintain in real life. In cyberspace you get to edit everything you say, no one smells funny, and everyone is presenting the best version of themselves. Unfortunately, online personas are no match for the real thing.

If You Must

If you absolutely cannot resist the allure of a "You've Got Mail" relationship, at least follow some guidelines:

Online Dating Rules:

1. Don't lie in your profile or misrepresent yourself in any way. If you're not into long nature walks and haven't been a size 6 since 1995, be

honest. Play up the good parts and your favorite things about yourself, but try to avoid being misleading.

2. If you must post a photo, post a recent one that isn't a glamour shot. Don't include anyone else in your photo and post a variety if you like. If you post a sexy photo, you may attract the wrong kind of attention.

3. Don't call anyone your one and only until you live in the same city. They might have as many online girlfriends as you have online boyfriends. Real friends are more important than cyber friends.

4. Talk to the guy on the phone first before you meet him. Get as much information about him as possible, try to find someone who knows him, and figure out if he really does work for the company he says he does. Google him.

5. Don't over-think your online conversation and e-mails. Be yourself, don't be the funniest girl you've ever met or a competitive brainiac.

6. If you must meet, bring along a friend to watch your back. Meet in public, wear your normal clothes and expect that he's shorter, heavier and balder than he said he is.

7. If you ever date anyone online, you are no longer entitled to mock other personal postings of any kind, no matter how bizarre.

8. Don't lie to everybody about how you met, but come to terms with the fact that people like me are going to tease you. Sorry, that's just the way it is.

9. He's not your boyfriend until you live in the same town.

10. Be safe. You just can't spot crazy on the outside. It would be nice if there was a sort of tagging system available. Like sharks or dolphins.

Let's say you are one of the few who got through the awkward first meeting stage and seem to have a relationship possibility at hand. Here's your next problem. Being that you met online, you probably live far away from each other. Time to read the section on G.U.D.'s or Geographically UnDesirable Relationships. No man is your boyfriend until he lives in your same area code.

G.U.D.'s

If your relationship requires traveling for more than an hour, sorry honey, but you've found yourself a G.U.D. It is impossible to have a normal, healthy, functioning relationship with somebody you can't see everyday if you wanted to. G.U.D. is not good. G.U.D. is Geographically UnDesirable.

How in the world are you supposed to seriously date somebody who lives more than an hour away from you? It's just impractical. First of all, dating a man who lives far away costs way too much. With the current prices of gas and phone bills, that should be the first reason not to date a G.U.D. Secondly, when you're dating somebody who does not live within your day-to-day lifestyle, you have on your hands a "Vacationship". That's a dating-relationship situation that is inextricably tied to a vacation. Every time you see each other, someone is visiting and everyday life is put on hold. There is no reason to call a man your boyfriend if he can't drive you to the airport or feed your bird while you're out of town. What good is having an emotional commitment to somebody who you always have to prepare to see?

Let me explain. Say you have an out of town boyfriend and that you've never lived in the same area. Every time he comes to visit you or you go visit him, you better believe you're going to bring your best outfits, get your hair done and do your nails before he gets there. It's like having a vacation-boyfriend. They are not a part of your life unless you include them, and this means you can be easily excluded from less pleasant things in their life. What are the motivations for trust in a long distance relationship? Why would you live apart from each other if you want to be together? If it's really serious, there's no reason why you can't live in the same area. But even when he does move into town, your relationship will change.

This Girl's Life:

I had this boyfriend whom I met through mutual friends when he was visiting my town. I would go to his town to visit or he would come to my town nearly every weekend. We had a great time when we were together,

but we were both in school so neither of us could move. It was a relationship

of convenience for both of us because we could concentrate on school during

the week and then spend weekends together. Our phone bills and gas bills

were exorbitant, but we didn't care because we thought it was true love.

In retrospect, I must have been insane. Is it really true love when you just have a serious relationship on the weekend? I don't think it helped much that I also had a "during the week" boyfriend, so clearly I wasn't that serious with my out-of-towner. But the point is this: You'll be more committed to men who live in your area, and they only maintain the same commitment to you depending on your vicinity.

Maintaining G.U.D. relationships only work if you have lived in the same place at one time or another. Even those become suspect, because if you loved each other and wanted to get married, why move? Why set yourself up for a cheating disaster with someone who lives far away? G.U.D. relationships should be casual at best. That way, if one of you happens to move to the area as the other, then at least you can do so under the guise that you're not moving for your significant other.

How many times have you heard stories about girls who move to wherever their boyfriend moved and get dumped as soon as they get there?

This one's my personal favorite:

Madeline and her boyfriend Max met in Utah at school, although she wasn't a member of the LDS church. They fell in love, she was taking the missionary discussions, and everything seemed great. Max wanted to go to medical school, so he applied to a variety of schools and was accepted to a handful in various states. To Madeline's dismay, Max chose the school located furthest away on the East Coast. Tearfully, Madeline helped Max pack and sent him on his way, smothering him with kisses and promises of visits.

Within a few months, Madeline couldn't take it anymore and decided to move to the same city as Max because she thought they were going to get married. When she got there, Madeline didn't know anyone except Max, but Max had already established himself at school and made friends. Madeline didn't know what to do with herself, so she got a part-time nanny job. After a few weeks, Max dumped Madeline, packed her up, and sent her home with her tail between her legs. Poor Madeline.

If your boyfriend moves away, your relationship is over. End of story. Don't follow him because he's moving away for a reason. Don't, don't, don't follow him. If it's true love, he would have proposed to you and you could move together, otherwise, he just wants an easy way out. When he says, "I'm moving" you should hear, "We're through, goodbye!"

If you move, do him the courtesy of breaking up with him before you go or he'll resent you for moving and that'll bring a world of problems. Dating relationships are only applicable within telephone area codes. Avoid G.U.D. situations and it'll save you a lot of heartache.

Be in the Right Place

Being in the right place at the right time is one tool HF uses to work miracles in our lives. Ezra Taft Benson's advice to "place yourselves in a position to meet worthy men and be engaged in constructive activities"[xlii] gets to the heart of the location part of finding a spouse. If you're looking in the right places for a husband, you will be more likely to find a worthy one. At bars and on unemployment lines are not good places to meet men. Online or in the next state are also not ideal places to find men to date. Men are weaklings. If they discover that there are women making themselves available online or in another county, they easily succumb to the temptation of taking advantage of the situation. Remember, it was a man who said, "There's a sucker born every second." The Internet and long distance dating are great opportunities for men to sneak around. Don't set yourself up to get suckered.

Resources:

- Arthur Golden's Memoirs of a Geisha. Yes, it was made into a movie, but no, geishas are not "women of ill repute." There are great pointers about attracting men without saying a word. I don't know how it's possible that a man would know these secrets, but Golden nails it.

- Ezra Taft Benson, "To the Single Adult Sisters of the Church," Ensign, Nov. 1988

- M. Russell Ballard, "Be Strong in the Lord," Ensign, July 2004. Elder Ballard addresses wasting time and the Internet, among other pearls.

- Dr. David Givens' *Love Signals*. An interesting analysis of courtship and body language.

- www.zappos.com - Great resource for shoes, no real relevance to anything in this chapter.

- www.Hersheys.com – Again, irrelevant. But did you know you can order personalized chocolate cards? Delicious!

Good Girl Goal #14: Know How to Pick 'Em

Last week in Sunday School, Brother Emery was giving a lesson on picking your spouse. He asked the class, "What are some essential things someone looks for in a potential spouse?" Everyone had different answers: "You need to be attracted to them," cried one.

"Common interests!"

"A good family!"

"Spirituality!"

"Good Cook" a male voice boomed from the back pew.

One young woman shouted, "He's needs to be tall!" The list went on and on. We shouted out all kinds of necessities for a mate. We made a list for the ideal man: A man must have a good job, a good relationship with his mother, and all his hair. He would have to be athletic and in good physical shape, brilliant and hilarious, kind and spiritual. Finally, one lady in the back hollered, "Plays games! All sorts!"

Remember Jane and Michael Banks from Mary Poppins? The two spoiled children had been making their nanny's lives miserable for years, but they still had these requirements for their 'Perfect Nanny':

If you want this choice position

Have a cheery disposition

Rosy cheeks, no warts!

Play games, all sorts!

You must be kind, you must be witty

Very sweet and fairly pretty

Take us on outings, give us treats

Sing songs, bring sweets.[xliii]

During our lesson, we made an interesting error. We weren't making a list of things we absolutely needed, or were essential, in a husband; we were making a list of qualifiers we used to choose who we were going to date. Attractiveness, good family, cooking skills, common interests, etc. are all things that go into picking who we want to date, not necessary marry.

This subtle distinction can give you a lot of freedom. Every man you date is not going to end up being your husband, so quit being so picky about the ones you let take you out for a good time. If you let go of all the little things, like eye color preference and height, you might end up meeting men who are perfect for you. Consider everybody. You could find a husband in the most unexpected package, wearing the most hideous shoes. You are going to have to open a lot of packages before you pick the right one. President Kimball said:

> **'Soul mates' are fiction and an illusion; and while every young man and young woman will seek with all diligence and prayerfulness to find a mate with whom life can be most compatible and beautiful, yet it is certain that almost any good man and any good woman can have happiness and a successful marriage if both are willing to pay the price.[xliv]**

Finding a spouse that is compatible with you takes figuring out what features are important to you and your eternal progression.

Being perfectly fit, sculpted, Johnny-Depped and toned does not a good husband make. Frequently, super hot guys are absolutely worthless. Think about it: If a guy has been hot all his life, isn't he used to being treated like he's God's gift to women? Being treated like that often causes hot guys to lack in other personal development – they're used to getting by on their looks and often work less hard for things they want. Being physically hot can be the equivalent of being a spoiled rich kid; they're not used to working for what they want. Hot guys might be completely lacking in drive, sense of humor, and even a job. Further, they may think they're hotter than you and that egotism is not a good balance for a relationship.

This is not to say that you shouldn't date super hot guys. Date as many as you want. Date whomever you feel like, but when it comes to actually considering with whom you're going to marry, the things that make up a guy's exterior and personality are secondary to features that are essential to your eternal progression.

There are only four things you need in a husband. Throw away all your lists. Cross off everything physical – it was important in getting the two of you together, but it is not important in an actual husband. Your husband looks nothing like what you would expect him to look like. Many women are not even remotely physically attracted to their husbands until they are going to marry them. How do you know what true love looks like? Think of the guy you thought was appealing when you first moved into your ward. Imagine he gave a Sunday School lesson all about how women belong in the kitchen and education is wasted on them. Does he become less physically attractive? Absolutely. What if a less stunning guy taught a lesson and mentioned off-hand that he is a chocolate physicist and thinks women should buy as many shoes as their hearts desired? Instantly more attractive. When it comes to men, what they say and do is infinitely more important than what they look like. Our perception of men determines their hotness. Give him a chance to show you his personality and the man grows to be attractive.

Once you're going out with guys, you learn about their interests, career, family, social background and character. Those features of a man are important in dating, but they are not of paramount importance to choosing a husband. Even if a guy came from two incarcerated parents, a mobile home, works in sanitation, and likes to play badminton, he can still be an excellent husband if he has the Golden Formula of features that are important to getting married. In this section, we're going to break it down to bare bone essentials, so you can quickly assess and eliminate candidates.

"The Golden Formula for Spouse Selection"

1) Immovable Testimony

2) Work Ethic

3) Common World View

4) Worships the Ground on which You Walk

That's it. There's your man. He will make you happy.

Anything else you get is an extra blessing from the Lord and we'll talk about "The Extras" last. Anything your guy doesn't have from your original list isn't important. Mel Gibson, I'll tell you what women want. Men they can trust. Specifically, men they can trust to get them food, children, help them in their own personal progression and eventually help them get to heaven. It's **The Golden Formula for Spouse Selection,** and honey, it works.

Worships the Ground on which You Walk

I personally believe in the genetics of the whole marriage business. As much as we say we're interested in getting married for love and companionship, the foundations of these desires are genetic, interestingly outlined in *The Selfish Gene* by Richard Dawkins. First thing: perpetuation of the species. Our genes are programmed to make us want to pass them on. Going to need a man for that, specifically a man who thinks we're as hot as Manolo Blahniks. The man you marry must **Worship the Ground on Which You Walk.** This guy needs to want you to be the mother of his children and the owner of the hand he holds as he marches into heaven. He needs to be as invested in your personal growth and happiness as you are.

I know this guy Jared. He's a great catch. Jared dated dazzling Margot for about two years. Margot had a temple recommend and real job, a humanity helping one: she taught art to preschoolers. Margot had a great education. Jared was a dentist, had a temple recommend, and was very active in church. While they were dating, Margot discovered that Jared had a good family, decent place to live, of marriageable age. They looked great together,

Margot saw a few other guys, but was mostly interested in pursuing marriage with Jared. Right around their two-year anniversary of dating, they broke up.

See any problem with this scenario? What man in his right mind would date a girl for two years and not get married to her? The kind of man who for some reason did not think Margot was God's Gift to Men and All Living Things. Who's the dummy with her heart broken? Margot! Give a guy with a temple recommend and a good job six months to a year to get a ring. If he doesn't, sorry lass, "He's Just Not That Into You."

Having a husband who loves you truly, madly, and deeply is one pillar in the foundation of a happy marriage. No one in your life will be as important as your spouse so he better be convinced that you are the greatest woman on the planet. Your future husband will be your best friend, your business partner, your lova, the father of your children, your emotional support, and everything else one human being can be to another. When you marry in the temple, you will be one flesh and you will have your own eternal family. If you are considering marriage with a guy, ask him when he thinks would be a good date to get married. The only acceptable answer is, "Today." You can tell that your guy worships the ground on which you walk if he begs and pleads with you to allow him to be your husband.

Your Future Husband Worships the Ground on Which You Walk if He:

1) Includes Heavenly Father in your relationship.

2) Tries to be your best friend.

3) Remembers that you're both still growing.

4) Acknowledges that you can have different opinions.

5) Uses charitable communication to settle conflict.

6) Follows righteous principles in your relationship.[xlv]

7) Wants to marry you right this second and gives you a ring to prove it.

Having this foundation of absolute blind desire (spiritual, emotional, and intellectual before physical) becomes the underpinning of your union. If he loves you, he will not want to fight with you. If he loves you, he will never break your heart. If he loves you, he will love your children. If he loves you, he will trust your judgment and honor you. President GBH counsels men:

Husbands, see in your wives your most valued asset in time or eternity, each a daughter of God, a partner with whom you can walk hand in hand, through sunshine and storm, through all the perils and triumphs of life.[xlvi]

If the man you marry sees you as his "most valued asset in time or eternity" he will understand his responsibility to treat you as such. The man you marry should be clawing to marry you – you are doing him a favor, so don't settle for anyone who doesn't Worship the Ground on Which You Walk! He should thank his lucky stars if you accept.

Work Ethic

Let's say your guy thinks you're more wonderful than Christmas. He's dying to marry you, wants you to have his 2.5 children. Pause a moment and think ahead! Once you're pregnant, a girl's gotta eat. So do her children. Does he have enough motivation to put bread on the table while you're waddling around with a basketball for a stomach? Basic hunter-gatherer theory here. We're going to need a man with a good work ethic and the ability to provide for a family for an indeterminate amount of time. He doesn't need to make a lot of money, but he has to have the potential to support a family if you decide to stay home and raise the children.

Eloise loved this boy Asher. Asher had everything Eloise wanted in a husband: he was spiritual and sweet; HF had even included some extras features like soft lips and hard abs. Eloise and Asher sat together through all the church meetings and frequently had interesting discussions about religious ideology, politics and the upcoming summer Grecian sandal trend. Asher left love notes on Eloise's car. When they were together he treated Eloise like a princess. Asher spent a few of his evenings at work as a caddie at the golf course. He would go on errands for Eloise, do all of his church work, and even play with her little brother, all before Eloise got home from work.

They broke up.

Problem? Asher didn't have a real job or any interest in pursuing a career that could support his family. Asher had very little **work ethic**. You can't be a part-time caddie and support a family. Eloise's genes just couldn't stand for that.

I do not believe that men need to be rich or even have a dime to their name. They can be debt ridden and penniless, but if the reasons are clear and there is a defined goal in mind, finances should be no impediment to marriage. Men frequently believe that they should wait until they have a little money in their pockets before they commit to marriage. If he has good work ethic and the potential to support a family, tell him he can buy you a fake diamond engagement ring. You can always upgrade later. **Work ethic** is infinitely more valuable than cash.

Having a clear plan in mind for their career and finances is a requirement. Your future husband, no matter how old he is, should be working in or towards his career. What you've learned applies to your man: No one is going to make his life successful but him. Work ethic is easy to evaluate: all you need to do is ask your guy his 20-year plan. If his 20-year plan involves buying a Playstation and taking a yoga class in Phuket, he may not have sufficient work ethic. Ask him what he wants to be doing in five years, ten, and twenty. Of course, all men think they're going to be rich. Rich is not important. Stable is important. Having hobbies is fine, but having definite goals and a plan for how to achieve those goals demonstrates an understanding of work ethic. In practice, **men with good work ethics do something every working day that either furthers their career goals or generates a steady income**. Men with good work ethic are unsatisfied with dead-end jobs and they plan to be the main source of income for their families (if possible). If they are working toward a goal and can keep a steady job, they will be more likely to continue working towards eternal family progression.

Since the seventies, the work world has been shaken up by women. Yes, we can absolutely provide the financial support for our families. No, this does not give men license to be loafers. Lots of men are artists and genuinely believe that they can support themselves and their families through their art. This includes film-makers, musicians, and freelance artists of all kinds. Unfortunately, when HF was handing out the personality attributes, I think He thought it would be clever to give some people tons of artistic ability and no self marketing skills. Artists are often bad at self-promotion (to anyone other than their loved ones, bless 'em). Lots of men think women are "dream killers," which means that their girlfriends and wives demand that they pursue traditional employment. If the guy you're dating is waiting tables during the week and playing gigs on the weekends, he is not living up to his potential. There is no reason why your guy shouldn't pursue a traditional career along with his artistic hobby. As soon as the hobby becomes lucrative and offers financial stability, the traditional career can go. Men who tread career water while being artists are hamstringing themselves – why not encourage them to add some career-oriented work experience to their resume?

There is no reason to crush your man's boyhood dreams. Men never grow up, girls like shoes. That's just the way things go. Every man still believes that he could have been a starting quarterback on a professional football team, that's why you see all those old men playing in Turkey Bowls on Thanksgiving. Praise them up and down for their talents and encourage them to pursue their talents either as a hobby or a real career. Believe in them and help them realize their dreams in a productive way, but don't get sucked into being a sugar mama. Help them set realistic goals and be willing to support them for an agreed upon amount of time. For example, if your guy is convinced that he needs to be an un-paid intern at a magazine in order to pursue a career in sports writing, tell him that you'd be happy to pay the bills for a year while he works toward his goal. A year should be sufficient to either solidify a paid career path with their dream, or go back to the drawing board. Your guy needs to feel worthy of your respect; this respect is earned by providing for you and your children. Without a great **work ethic**, it will be hard for you to respect him and for him to respect himself.

Immovable Testimony

Maybe the guy ranking highest in your dating pool is in business school and worships the ground on which you walk. Great, so you'll have a well-fed family. What to do with them? Probably going to love them a lot. Probably want to get them into heaven.

Aviva is my friend from college. She had an outstanding boyfriend, Cooper. He bought Aviva flowers. She made Cooper dinner. Cooper worked high up in Hollywood as a script doctor. Aviva was working on being a Social Worker. Great families, both of them. They dated for nearly a year, and Cooper was head over heels in love with Aviva. They both wanted to travel the world and adopt at least one child from South America. They loved existential debates about the existence of God. One day Aviva was dreaming of all the extraordinary places Cooper would take her. The next day, they broke up.

Problem? He was a card carrying atheist! (See rule # 1: **Immovable Testimony**) C'mon ladies! You do this all the time! We're all guilty of it, but we stick around dating these men who don't have any potential to be our husbands.

If we keep dating guys like this, we're going to be forty and unmarried, maxing out all our established credit on Botox!

How do you determine whether or not your man has an immovable testimony? Ask him! Communicate! Discuss with him his past callings and how they affected his life. He doesn't have to have gone on a mission, but he should explain his reasons for not going and you need to find them acceptable. If he's of mission age, encourage him to go serve the Lord on a full time mission. Whether you get married or not, he'll be thankful for life.

Ask if he's ever been inactive from church or disfellowshiped. Have him talk to you about the Priesthood and his expectations for how it will be used in your home, as well as how often he intends to attend the temple. Don't expect any more from your husband's faith than you do from your own, but do expect that you're of equal strength and can help each other when one of you is having obedience problems. Does he wear his garments? Does he use the Priesthood? Talk to him about all areas that pertain to faithful worship, and don't leave out the hard stuff like pornography or the Word of Wisdom. It's a little bit evil, but you could even test him if you wanted to by telling him you don't feel like going to church that week. See how he responds. Your future husband should encourage the best out of you and have high standards for his own gospel activity. Think up problematic scenarios and ask how he would respond. Research your man until you are satisfied that his testimony and dedication to the gospel is unshakeable. Heavenly Father must be included in your relationship if you intend to have a successful marriage.

The Gospel teaches us that married women can't leave their husbands in the dust and take their kids into the celestial kingdom. You need the Priesthood in your life; your children need the Priesthood in their home. Don't shortchange your children a worthy priesthood example or you will regret it. Marry for the first time in the temple – please don't do the low commitment thing and get married secularly with the intentions of being sealed later. Secular weddings by LDS Bishops are no frills operations because you're not sealed forever. "What therefore God hath joined together, let not man put asunder."[xlvii] You will feel cheated and your marriage will lack the foundation and blessings of the temple if you don't marry in the temple right off the bat. There will be an implicit trust fortified by the temple blessings that will be a well of strength in your marriage.

You need to be able to count on your companion to help you if you're having difficulty with the gospel standards. Is this guy going to help you through it toward obedience or convince you that you shouldn't worry about letting your standards slip a little? Marriage is a partnership, a team effort, and the easiest way to win is to be playing the same game. Some think that wives get into heaven on the coattails of their husbands, that we need men to get through the gates, but I tend to think it's the other way around. We do them the charity of letting them escort us there, as long as they have immovable testimonies.

Common World View

But what are you going to do in the years between popping out a few of his children and knocking on the pearly gates? You're going to be living with somebody. You better have the same idea about the way the world works and your place within it. What if your husband had a great testimony, work ethic, and loved you dearly but was raised to think that men don't do housework? That's a recipe for disaster! No, you're going to *have* to make sure you have the same world view and that you see the world through the same lens.

This Girl's Life:

Before I was married, I went online and tried to find compatibility tests for my boyfriends and me to take. When my future husband finally came on the scene, I did the same. Our zodiac signs don't match up at all. Neither do our Color Code colors nor our Chinese Horoscope. And yet, we have happily functional and loving marriage because we have the same world view: we expect the same things out of life. I expect that he will be employed; he expects that I will raise his children. He expects that I will do my calling; I expect that he will honor the Priesthood. I expect that he will stay awake until one in the morning if I don't make him go to sleep, and he expects that I will secretly shop for shoes on E-bay. We understand what we want from each other.

Having the same world view is pretty simple and it's entertaining to explore. It's all about questioning and getting to know one another. Test him out; see what the guy believes before you meet him at the temple.

Potential Spouse Discussion Topics

Who does which chores? Is one person responsible for the same chore all the time?

Early bird or night owl?

How do you expect to spend your holidays?

When do you want to have kids?

What do you want to accomplish in 5, 10, 20, 50 years?

How do you feel about the things I want to accomplish in 5, 10, 20, 50 years?

What traditions are you used to incorporating?

How is money handled? Do you budget or spend?

What do you think is a reasonable amount to spend on food, trips, play, shoes?

What's a week of marriage going to look like with you?

What happens if one of us loses our job?

How will you handle church callings?

Do you have any seriously conflicting political views?

How do you live the gospel?

What about sexual behaviors?

How and when do you plan to raise children?

This is just a short list of the types of things that make up a world view. Here's the thing with the **Common World View**: you have to want the same things. You have to be interested in some of the same activities, share some of the same goals. You don't have to be the exact same person, but it's important that you accept the person you have in front of you, not who he's going to be in five years. You have to appreciate each other's sense of humor. Maybe you've read the same books (other than just the Scriptures). You have to understand the gospel in the same way. Even when people live the gospel, which is an explicit series of standards and expectations, individuals live it differently and understand the same principles through their own personal perspective. Intentions for money, parenting, goals, and daily life need to be discussed. Talk about EVERYTHING.

Write down your 5-year, 10-year, and 20-year plans. Do they match? And don't be generic: everybody has marriage and two kids on their list. Write a list of ten specific things you want to accomplish in your life. Do you actually want to be with someone while they're accomplishing those things? Do you respect each other's profession? Be honest – would you still love him if he were out of work and sitting on your couch playing video games for three months? Quit fooling yourself and trying to talk yourself into liking him. This one's crucial: have you ever been embarrassed of him in a social situation? Get out now. It only gets worse.

This Girl's Life:

I had this one sweetheart of a boyfriend, Oliver. We got along really well; he had an immovable testimony and was steadily progressing in his profession. Oli and I had been dating on and off for nearly six months when my Uncle Anthony came into town and offered to take us both out to dinner. I was excited to show off Oliver because I thought he was charming and interesting. I didn't see Uncle Anthony very frequently because he lived far away in Maryland. Nonetheless, Anthony and I got along well and his opinion mattered a great deal to me.

While we were at the restaurant, Uncle Anthony and I were chatting it up. Oliver sat silent. Occasionally, Uncle Anthony would ask Oliver a question to try to get him talking, but Oliver would answer quickly and fall

silent again. Eventually, Uncle Anthony gave up and Oli just stared off into

space. It was one of the longest meals of my life.

When I asked Oli what was wrong during the meal, he said

genuinely that he thought everything was fine. I was perplexed. After much

discussion, I realized that Oliver only turns on the charm when he thinks it

would be useful. Oli didn't see the need to impress my Uncle. He was bored

and didn't mind conveying that attitude. Unfortunately, I believe in being

conversational to everybody, whether they're useful to me or not. I thought

Oli was being unkind, he thought he was being normal.

Differing social expectations is just one way world view affects our lives. If you're dating a variety of men, observe which ones you take to which activities. The one with whom you feel most comfortable in an assortment of social situations is probably the guy for you. I knew my husband was the right guy for me when I could trust him to carry his side of the conversation, no matter if we were among my coworkers, a crowd of ex-boyfriends, or my Uncle Anthony. We had the same social expectations.

Another thing that can cause problems in marriages if it's not discussed beforehand is expectations about sex. Once you are engaged, it is perfectly acceptable to discuss in a non-titillating way what your lines are sexually. You want to know what you're signing up for, though most things can be handled once you're hitched. I personally believe in full disclosure, but you can consult with your bishop on this.

Doing relationship reconnaissance is critical in choosing your mate. Don't go into this thing blind. Horoscopes are fun, and maybe the world is ordered in one of those obscure ways, but if the month you were born in is the only thing you have in common, start looking for the green exit sign.

Before you marry this guy, it's okay to be a bit of a sleuth. Google his name and see brick and mortar of the building where he says he works. Meet coworkers, family members (even the embarrassing ones), and maybe even snoop around his computer for pornography. Ask for a half-hour alone in his room unattended, ala MTV's Room Raiders. Meet someone who has known him for more than two years. Look him up at the college he says he attended. This is the job interview of a lifetime; get the facts before you offer him the position. Make sure this guy isn't just putting on an elaborate show to convince you that his life and world view are up to par.

To be fair, however, as much as we plan, pick and choose, sometimes you just can't control who you like. Maybe he is a little embarrassing, but he's perfect in every other way. It's mystical; if you like him, you like him. But you need to be prepared to quickly give the boot to the ones you like if they don't have the **Golden Formula for Spouse Selection**. You're just going to waste your time. Dating a guy for three to six months should be enough to figure him out, test him against the formula and promote him or fire him. If he gets four stars on the Golden Formula, then the other little things are not that important. Some personality features are just part of a guy's character, part of his charm – don't try to change them now or ever. He doesn't have to be perfect, but if he has the Golden Formula, you need to consider him for marriage. If you would be kicking yourself for the rest of your life for not marrying this guy, then it's time to start taking the relationship seriously.

The Extras

Most of the requirements you had on your list from childhood were things like honesty, romance, good with children, blonde hair, an SUV, and a six-figure salary, etc. All of these things are either extras or covered by the Golden Formula. If you wait for a husband who has an immoveable testimony, then you will get your honest husband because anyone with a secure testimony tries to live the laws of the gospel. If you want a husband who is good with children, you will get one if you marry a man who worships the ground on which you walk.

When you're buying shoes, the first requirement they must follow is function. Shoes must first protect your feet from the pavement, match your outfit and look appropriate to the event where you need to wear them. Anything other than those requirements (like height of heel, color, and details) are all extra features. Function is first, preference is second or not important. The following list has on the right side the features (or functions) you'll have if you marry someone with the Golden Formula for Spouse Selection. The left side lists extra things that might be nice, but don't really matter.

Husband Requirements: Necessities and Extras

Necessities covered by following The Golden Formula	Extra Features, not that important if they don't have the Golden Formula
Loves the Lord	Physical packaging: height, weight, eye color, muscle tone, a.k.a "Johnny Depping"
Eye single to the Glory of God	He's the coolest or most popular guy at school or church.
He supports you emotionally and spiritually.	He has a bulging bank account
Has a current Temple Recommend	He owns a house and hot car.
Understands you / Sense of Humor (result of common world view)	He's the life of the party. (More important that he makes you the star.)
Real romance: Respect and Adoration	Passion and movie-like romance
Kindness, Integrity, and Wisdom	Your taste in art, music, movies, and theater. (You can grow together.)

Wants and loves children (will love your children)	You LOVE his family.
Gets a Paycheck	Socioeconomic status of his family. (Remember the widow who tithed a penny, money doesn't determine righteousness.)

This Girl's Life:

When I realized I was going to marry my husband it was not that much of a surprise. It wasn't one of those heart goes pitter-pat things and I'll tell you why. I was completely rational while I made the biggest and best decision of my life; the most romance I have ever experienced was when I realized that someone loved me, expected the best from me, and was going to push me to live up to my potential.

The daily life of marriage may not be terribly exciting, just like being a member of a family isn't amazingly interesting on a day to day basis. What marriage and family lacks in bouquets of flowers and exotic vacations, it makes up for in the everyday comfort of knowing that you're loved, flaws and all. We'd met each other's families, we'd talked about everything we expected from life, and being around him felt like being around a friend I had known for years, though we'd only been dating about three months. I was just thinking about him one day and I decided that I would be an absolute fool not to marry him.

He had the four things I required for a husband. And about a thousand other extras.

An **immoveable testimony, work ethic, common world view,** and having him **worship the ground on which you walk** are the four things you absolutely need in a man. In fact, I think they qualify that man as a good man. Now take a look back on all of your boyfriends. How many of them had all four? Yeah, that's what I thought. You can't say for sure that any one of them had a Yatzee. If one of them did, you'd be married.

Resources:

- Salynn Boyles, "What Makes Wives Happy? Both New and Old Ideas of Marriage."[xlviii] Online article regarding WebMD report of marriage study, March 2006

- Thomas S. Monson, "Hallmarks of a Happy Home," Ensign, Nov. 1988, 69

- Thomas B. Holman, "Choosing and Being the Right Spouse," Ensign, Sept. 2002, 62

- Robert K. McIntosh *How do You Know when You're Really in Love?* This little manual by an LDS author has checklists and things to look for in your relationship. It's fun.

- Susan Piver's *The Hard Questions: 100 Essential Questions to Ask the One You Love*. Excellent questions for reconnaissance.

- Taylor Hartman's *The Color Code*. Entertaining way to categorize personality types.

- Heavenly Father. When in doubt, pray and ask Him if He really expects you to spend the rest of your life with this guy. When it's right, HF will let you know and you will have no doubts.

Conclusion

Okay, ladies! What have we learned? Are you the best woman for the job of marriage? Do you now have an idea of how to gain a full well of experience? Do you have clear educational goals and a career map? Are you constantly evaluating the substance of your testimony? Have you warded off your nosy mother with marriage statistics and weeded out the ineligible in the garden of single men? Are your twenties set to be years of self-fulfillment and glorious Singlehood? Have you realized that when your life gives you confidence, you are the most radiant and attractive woman on the planet?

Do you strut like the confident woman you are?[xlix]

Well, maybe you're not all of those things right now this very second. All of the *Good Girl Goals* should be on your To Do List, but the most important thing you should be doing with your twenties is TRYING. I hope you caught that theme in this guide – trying to live the will of the Lord is the first step toward being happy. You may not have all your goals completed, but that's okay. As long as you want righteous things and are trying to attain them, you're doing pretty well. In the April 2006 Sunday Morning Session of General Conference, Elder Holland refers to Alma 32:27 which reminds us that trying is a foundational principle of the gospel living:

"If ye can no more than desire to believe," Alma says, exercising just "a particle of faith," giving even a small place for the promises of God to find a home—that is enough to begin. Just believing, just having a "molecule" of faith—simply hoping for things which are not yet seen in our lives, but which are nevertheless truly there to be bestowed—that simple step, when focused on the Lord Jesus Christ, has ever been and always will be the first principle of His eternal gospel, the first step out of despair.[1]

Taking steps toward Christ are good steps, even if they're just little baby steps. Everything you do with the intentions of making yourself ready for marriage is a step toward eternal life. Christ will bless those who desire to believe.

By now you might be saying, "Wait a second, I now know all this stuff but you haven't told me when I will get married. Don't I need to plan for THAT?!!" Well, no. Regarding the timing of our marriage, President Dallin H. Oaks said:

The timing of marriage is perhaps the best example of an extremely important event in our lives that is almost impossible to plan. Like other important mortal events that depend on the

agency of others or the will and timing of the Lord, marriage cannot be anticipated or planned with certainty.[li]

And there you go. We can't really plan for it but in the meantime we need to perfect ourselves. The scriptures promise that the Lord will step in to help us towards our eternal progression, only after we have done all that we can do. We must prepare ourselves to be wives and mothers. We make ourselves the best candidates for temple marriage by carefully putting all areas of our lives are in order. The reward for our efforts is immeasurable – to go to the house of the Lord to create a new and everlasting eternal family. While we are doing our part, God will do the rest in His own time.

I know that God has a plan for every one of us. I'm thankful for a world that is rife with opportunities to be happy and gain life experience. I love being a woman and living in the fullness of times. Women are divine creatures of Heavenly Father, our lives can be blessed beyond our wildest imaginations if we live according to the gospel and strive towards eternal progression. I know that Christ is our living Redeemer that He loves us, and He delights in our happiness. I am thankful for free agency and the Atonement.

I believe that every woman is unique and chosen to live at this time. Where much is given, much is required. While we educate and perfect ourselves we are counseled to hold tightly to the iron rod so that we might claim the blessing of temple marriage and eternal life.

In D&C 101:16 Jesus Christ counsels, "Be still and know that I am God." Your Heavenly Father has a plan for you; your eternal companion will show up according to God's schedule. You owe it to yourself to be happy 'til your guy gets here. Now go and try to be a *Good Girl*.

Appendix 1

Estimated Median Age at First Marriage, 4-Year Average: 200-2003		
	Estimated Median Age At First Marriage	
Area	Men	Women
Average in United States	26.7	25.1
Alabama	25.5	23.8
Alaska	25.7	22.8
Arizona	26.1	24.5
Arkansas	25.0	22.8
California	27.2	25.2
Colorado	26.4	24.4
Connecticut	28.9	26.4
Delaware	27.0	25.5
D.C.	30.1	29.9
Florida	27.1	25.2
Georgia	26.3	24.4
Hawaii	27.8	25.7
Idaho	24.6	22.8

Illinois	27.0	25.5
Indiana	26.1	24.4
Iowa	25.9	24.5
Kansas	25.5	24.4
Kentucky	25.3	22.8
Louisiana	26.0	24.8
Maine	26.6	25.6
Maryland	27.1	25.8
Massachusetts	29.1	27.4
Michigan	27.1	25.6
Minnesota	26.6	25.2
Mississippi	25.8	24.8
Missouri	25.8	24.7
Montana	26.2	24.5
Nebraska	26.0	24.4
Nevada	26.3	23.7
New Hampshire	27.2	25.7
New Jersey	28.6	26.4

New Mexico	25.9	24.4
North Carolina	28.9	27.0
North Carolina	25.8	24.5
North Dakota	26.9	25.0
Ohio	26.6	25.2
Oklahoma	24.9	22.7
Oregon	26.6	24.6
Pennsylvania	27.6	25.9
Rhode Island	27.6	26.7
South Carolina	26.4	25.2
South Dakota	25.8	24.3
Tennessee	25.7	24.0
Texas	25.7	23.5
Utah	23.9	21.9
Vermont	27.8	25.9
Virginia	27.0	25.0
Washington	26.5	24.9
West Virginia	25.9	23.9

Wisconsin	26.9	25.5
Wyoming	25.7	23.3

Note: For the median age estimates shown in this table, 0.1 years provides the margin of error for each median age at the 90-percent confidence interval.

Source: U.S. Census Bureau, American Community Survey 2002-2003, Census Supplementary Survey 2000-2001. [lii]

Endnotes

[i] Genesis 29:17. See all of Genesis 29 and 30 for Rachel's story.

[ii] Genesis 29:11.

[iii] Sydney Smith Reynolds, "Wife and Mother: A Valid Career Option for the College-Educated Woman," *Ensign*, Oct. 1979, 67, paraphrased.

[iv] Attributed to Mae West.

[v] Maltin, Liza Jane "First Marriages Often End in Divorce" WebMD Medical News <http://my.webmd.com/content/article/32/1728_80368?src=Inktomi&condition=Home%20&%20Top%20Stories> Accessed January 30, 2007.

[vi] Gordon B. Hinckley, "Stand True and Faithful," *Ensign*, May 1996, 91.

[vii] Boyles, Salynn, "What Makes Wives Happy? Both New and Old Ideas of Marriage, Study Shows" Medicine Net.com, <http://www.medicinenet.com/script/main/art.asp?articlekey=60248> Accessed March 20, 2006.

[viii] 'California Community Colleges System' Wikipedia, <http://en.wikipedia.org/wiki/California_Community_Colleges_system> Accessed January 4, 2007.

[ix] Gordon B. Hinckley, *Ensign*, Nov. 1998, 51.

[x] All College Data in this section from <http://www.usnews.com/usnews/edu/college/rankings/rankindex_brief.php> Accessed September 22, 2006.

[xi] 'Statistical Highlights' Brigham Young University Graduation <http://saas.byu.edu/depts/graduation/statistics.aspx> Accessed July 13, 2006.

[xii] If you're moving to Boston or New York City, their rental arrangements are extremely difficult and costly because they use realtors. It's a mess. Look out.

xiii Howard W. Hunter, "Prepare for Honorable Employment," *Ensign*, Nov. 1975, 122.

xiv Ezra Taft Benson, "Pay Thy Debt, and Live" *Ensign*, June 1987, 3.

xv Howard W. Hunter, "Prepare for Honorable Employment," *Ensign*, Nov. 1975, 122.

xvi According to wikipedia.com, A hobo is a migratory worker; a tramp is a migratory non-worker; a bum is a non-migratory non-worker.

xvii Don O. Ostler, "Keeping Our Balance: Recognizing and Resisting Excesses," *Tambuli*, Jan. 1983, 27. (Quoting Joseph F. Smith)

xviii Gordon B. Hinckley, "To Single Adults," *Ensign*, June 1989, 72.

xix Ibid.

xx Derbyshire, David, "Daytime Nap 'is as refreshing as night's sleep'" Telegraph, June 23, 2003. <http://www.telegraph.co.uk/news/main.jhtml?xml=/news/2003/06/23/wnap23.xml&sSheet=/portal/2003/06/23/ixportal.html>

xxi 1 Nephi 13:37.

xxii James E. Faust, "Womanhood: The Highest Place of Honor," *Ensign*, May 2000, 95.

xxiii Gordon B. Hinckley, "Some Thoughts on Temples, Retention of Converts, and Missionary Service," *Ensign*, Nov. 1997, 49.

xxiv Richard G. Scott, "Why Every Member a Missionary?" *Ensign*, Nov. 1997.

xxv Jeffrey R. Holland, "Personal Purity," *Ensign*, Nov. 1998, 75.

xxvi "The Family: A Proclamation to the World" read by Gordon B. Hinckley as part of his message at the General Relief Society Meeting held September 23, 1995.

xxvii Jeffrey R. Holland, "Personal Purity," *Ensign*, Nov. 1998, 75 quoting 1Corinthians 6:18 and Doctrine & Covenants 59:6, emphasis added.

xxviii Spencer W. Kimball, 'The Time to Labor Is Now," *Ensign*, November 1975, 7.

xxix Bruce Monson, "Speaking of Kissing," *New Era*, June 2001, 32.

xxx 'Statistics' Rape, Abuse, & Incest National Network.
<http://www.rainn.org/statistics/index.html> Accessed January 15, 2007.

xxxi Spencer W. Kimball in Conference Report, Sydney Australia Area Conference 1976, 54.

xxxii Neal A. Maxwell, "The Seventh Commandment: A Shield," *Ensign*, Nov. 2001, 78.

xxxiii Stephen Levitt, *Freakonomics: A Rogue Economist Explores the Hidden Side of Everything* (New York: Penguin Group, 2005) paraphrasing findings in Rolf Loeber and Magda Stouthamer-Loeber, "Family Factors as Correlates and Predictors of Juvenile Conduct Problems and Delinquincy," *Crime and Justice*, vol. 7, ed Michael Tonry and Norval Morris (Chicago: University Press, 1986)., William S. Comanor and Llad Phillips, "The Impact of Income and Family Structure on Delinquincy," University of California – Santa Barbara working paper, 1999., and Pijkko Rasanen et al., "Maternal Smoking During Pregnancy and Risk of Criminal Behavior Among Adult Male Offspring in Northern Finland 1966 Birth Cohort," *American Journal of Psychiatry* 156 (1999), 857-62.

xxxiv 'America's Children in Brief: Key National Indicators of Well-Being, 2006' Forum on Child and Family Statistics.
<http://www.childstats.gov/americaschildren/index.asp> Accessed January 3, 2007.

xxxv 'Make-up,' Oxford English Dictionary Online, <//http://dictionary.oed.com/>. Accessed March 27, 2006

xxxvi Gladwell, Malcolm, *Blink: The Power of Thinking Without Thinking* Little, Brown and Company, 2005.

xxxvii Job 31:15.

xxxviii 'Fashion,' English Dictionary Online, <//http://dictionary.oed.com/>. Accessed March 27, 2006.

xxxix Boyd K. Packer "Ye Are the Temple of God" Sunday Afternoon Conference Session, October 8, 2000. (Quoting Harold B. Lee)

xl Glenn L. Pace, "Confidence and Self-Worth," *Ensign,* Jan. 2005, 32.

xli LeGrand R. Curtis, "Searching for the One You Will Marry," *New Era*, June 1993, 4.

xlii Ezra Taft Benson, "To the Single Adult Sisters of the Church," *Ensign*, Nov. 1988, 96.

xliii Sherman, Richard G *Mary Poppins Enhanced Soundtrack*, Disney, 2004.

xliv Spencer W. Kimball, *Marriage and Divorce* (1976), 16.

xlv Rules 1-6 inspired by Janette K. Gibbons, "Seven Steps to Strengthen a Marriage," *Ensign*, March 2002.

xlvi Gordon B. Hinckley, "What God Hath Joined Together," *Ensign*, May 1991, 71.

xlvii Matt. 19:6.

xlviii Boyles, Salynn, "What Makes Wives Happy? Both New and Old Ideas of Marriage, Study Shows" Medicine Net.com, <http://www.medicinenet.com/script/main/art.asp?articlekey=60248> Accessed March 20, 2006.

xlix One of the worst movies ever made (and also one of my favorites) is *Staying Alive* starring John Travolta. It's meant to be a sequel to *Saturday Night Fever* (rated R, I only saw the PG edited television version) and *Staying Alive* is the story of Tony five years later. Tony (Travolta) tries to make it as a dancer on Broadway. The only redeemable part of the movie is the end when Travolta, having conquered Broadway, asks his friend, "You know what I wanna do?" His friend replies, "What?" Travolta replies, "Strut." The movie closes with Travolta pounding the pavement with the most distinctively confident strut ever recorded on film. It's beautiful.

l Jeffrey R. Holland, "Broken Things to Mend," General Conference, April 2006.

li Dallin H. Oaks, "Timing," *Liahona*, Oct. 2003, 10.

lii http://www.census.gov/population/www/socdemo/fertility/slideshow/table01.xls

www.ingramcontent.com/pod-product-compliance
Lightning Source LLC
Chambersburg PA
CBHW031244090426
42742CB00007B/305